A Prostitute

No Longer

Rev. Lisa R. Pate

Copyright © 2021 Rev. Lisa R. Pate

ISBN: 978-1-7379706-0-6

All rights reserved. No part of this publication may be reproduced, distributed, or transmitted in any form or by any means, including photocopying, recording, or other electronic or mechanical methods, without the prior written permission of the publisher, except in the case of brief quotations embodied in critical reviews and certain other noncommercial uses permitted by copyright law. For permission requests, contact Rev. Lisa R. Pate at Lrpate@listeningearpublications.com.

Any references to historical events, real people, or real places are used and names have been changed to protect their identity.

Front cover image by Rev. Lisa R. Pate

Editing and formatting and design by Katie Erickson

First published in 2021 in the United States.

Scripture quotations marked NLT are taken from the *Holy Bible*, New Living Translation, copyright © 1996, 2004, 2015 by Tyndale House Foundation. Used by permission of Tyndale House Publishers, Inc., Carol Stream, Illinois 60188. All rights reserved.

Scripture quotations marked NKJV are taken from the New King James Version. Copyright © 1982 by Thomas Nelson, Inc. Used by permission. All rights reserved.

www.listeningearpublications.com

Dedication

This book is dedicated to Cornelius (Cornel), April, Israel, Caleb & my grandchildren, Mylessa Anne & Riley Owen

Thank you to my heartbeat, my firstborn son, Cornel. The day I left you with a crack-pipe in my hand, I died. Yet you loved me past my hurt, guilt, and shame. God heard the longing in our hearts for one another and brought us back together. I truly treasure the joys that we now share as a family together. You are now 38 years old. You've granted me access back into your life and into your heart, and for that I am eternally grateful! To your beautiful wife April, God's chosen vessel for you, my granddaughter Mylessa Ann and our youngest heart's prayer, Riley Owen, you all are the light in my lamp.

To the two wonders in my world, Israel and Caleb – You both are like air and water to me. I need you both to live. When I wanted to crawl inside of my box filled with mistakes, rejection and, regret, your care pulled me out of that box and made me live and move, growing from striving to surviving and finally to thriving! You and your love for me have proven and shown me God's true forgiveness and the ability to start life over and live again.

The Layers of Life

Endorsements 1
Foreword 3
Introduction 5

How Did I Get There?

Layer One ~ Daddy, Keep Silent 9
Layer Two ~ Father to the Fatherless 17
Layer Three ~ Delayed Growth 33
Layer Four ~ Unhealthy Exposure 47

Why I Stayed There

Layer Five ~ Self Esteem 57
Layer Six ~ Shame, Rejection, and Guilt 72
Layer Seven ~ FEAR 113
Layer Eight ~ Perfect Pride 123

How I Moved from There

Layer Nine ~ Free Indeed 133
Trust My Silence 143
Lastly Spoken 147

Acknowledgements 149
References 155

Endorsements

This book is a must-read for anyone who appreciates the power of a great comeback. You will find yourself immersed as Rev. Lisa Pate paints a vivid picture of redemption at its finest. As she walks you through a transparent unfolding of her early life, she helps you appreciate how the challenges of her past catalyzed the birthing of God's supernatural plans for her future. Her story will not only resonate with many who feel limited because of their troubled background, but it will revive hope in anyone who wishes to join the journey of healing and freedom in Christ.

– Bishop James and Rev. Tiffaney Izzard

Rev. Lisa Pate shows pure transparency in her book *A Prostitute No Longer*! The details of her life are raw but honest. It will remind you that God sees all you go through and has never left you or forgotten about you. Each layer (chapter) gives Scripture references that support the hope she shares. Read this book and learn from someone who has experienced much darkness but chooses to walk in the light of God's love.

– Bishop Ricky A. Felton
Senior Pastor
Life Builders Church of God

In the book *A Prostitute No Longer*, Rev. Lisa Pate takes readers on an amazing adventure from dark places in her life to her current place of hope, love, acceptance, and wholeness. As you read it, layers of hurt, pain, and embarrassment are peeled away. There were times I had to stop reading because the pain became personal for me. But after praying and reflecting on the hope that fills her story, I was excited to continue reading. By the end of the book, you will have experienced true freedom – freedom to live a life of completeness that's only found in Christ. This is a must-read for anyone who needs hope and encouragement!

– Rev. Pat Felton
First Lady
Life Builders Church of God

Foreword

Reverend Lisa R. Pate is an Ordained Minister in the Church of God with International Offices located in Cleveland, Tennessee. Lisa was one of my congregants during my wife Janice and my last pastoral appointment at the Harvest Temple Church of God (now known as Life Builders Church of God), located in Forestville, Maryland. She is known for her compassionate care for the homeless, one who goes the second mile (Matthew 5:41) to reveal the greatness in others, and her willingness to make sacrifices for her children and family.

Lisa's book, *A Prostitute No Longer*, is an inspiring story of God's love and a reminder of my great-grandmother's love for making beautiful quilts for members of the family. My great-grandmother's quilts were woven from bits and pieces of cloths that were of no use to others, but through the eyes of this great woman's vision, each piece of cloth was someone's story and beautiful masterpiece that told a story while providing warmth, comfort, and joy to so many who would share the story of "strength from the unwanted."

Lisa's book is a confession of an uncut story that advocates the love of God and His grace to deliver men and women from sin through the cross of Calvary regardless of their life's history. Her story shows how God's love protects and cares for sinners until they recognize that there is more to life than sin and shame. Lisa's openness provides no room for uncertainty but brings clarity on how we can be lured into a spider's web, captured by the sense that we are stronger than the spider and would only be here for a moment until we are set free by God's grace. What she thought would be brief moments of time turned into an extended entrapment until she was covered with a seemly inescapable web. In this book, you will not find Lisa succumbing to being the victim or blaming anyone for her challenges; instead, she shares how with God's help she emerges from a place of victimology to an engrafted member of the Family of God with full rights to Kingdom awareness as an adopted daughter of God.

This book acknowledges the depths and paths of sin, yet Lisa shares how she accepted her faults and recognized her need for God's Spirit, willpower, and fortitude to overcome the grip of sin, and the need of God's Spirit to move her past the years of torment by the washing of the Word of God into a place of forgiveness with clarity that moved her to forward-thinking with a new name, called "HIS" (Ephesians 1:11-14). She allows the Holy Spirit of God the necessary time to complete His transformation in her and to process her ability and strength to pass the test or retake the test until she is fully delivered and willing to "wait for it," and be fully delivered, restored, and become a "testimony of change." She also meets you where you are, introduces Christ, testifies she has been in this low place too, and acknowledges it was Christ who pulled her up, out, and through to a life of victory.

This book is what I like to call a "divine exposure." She opens with transparency, shows you each piece of her life like the fragments of the quilt that seemed to have no worth, and then with heartfelt prayers, she compels you to identify those deeply hidden paths in your life that have not been revealed. She encourages you to face the fears that have held you captive in a web. With honesty and clarity, this book brings you face to face with your worst nightmares, challenges you to explore all the "what if's," and offers the confidence and resiliency to trust God to cover us like a quilt and allow us the opportunity to know His grace like Lisa and be exposed to a life of "New Beginnings that can only be experienced in Christ."

> Bishop (Dr.) Kenneth L. Hill, Administrative Bishop
> Church of God Cleveland Tennessee

Introduction

Have you ever looked at someone who was on the street begging for what seemed to be their very existence? Perhaps to you it seemed as though they were scratching and clawing for life, and you wondered, *how did they get there?* Maybe it did not bother you at all because that person was not someone you knew personally; sometimes it's not easy, but it's doable, to turn and look the other way when that person is a stranger and not connected to your life.

But what about when that person is someone you know quite well? Many, many years ago, I was that person. I was the one on the street begging and prostituting myself for my very existence. It doesn't look like it now because the Lord's covering is so amazing. God rescues His children out of the kingdom of darkness and transfers us into the Kingdom of His dear Son, whom He loves (Colossians 1:13). He cleans us up so well that we don't look like what we've been through; we don't even smell like the fire we came out of. This book and its companion devotional (A Prostitute No Longer ~ The Devotional©) are about what I've been through: my life on the street as a former crack cocaine addict, my experiences and lessons learned through being a prostitute, how I got there, why I stayed, and finally how I was delivered.

Since my return to Jesus Christ as my Lord and Savior, 26 years ago, I've dedicated my life to Him and my heart has been set apart for Kingdom purposes. Yet, as I continue to grow and develop as a Christian, I often see situations and circumstances where many confessing Christian believers are identifying, relating closely, and even partaking in the shady principles of my former lifestyle of prostitution. Really! How so, you ask? Well, I see many believers prostituting their anointing, their gifts, their talents, their time, and in some cases even themselves. I see many believers who I know love God operating in idolatry, knowingly or unknowingly. Nevertheless, it's my desire to bring light to these practices and be a vessel that God is using in this hour to trumpet righteousness, at every turn and most certainly at every cost.

Journey on with me and I will show you how.

How Did I Get There?

Layer One ~ Daddy, Keep Silent

"If you see Lila again, I'll kill you!" So the story goes about my father. He was married to another woman, and my mom was his girlfriend. The relationship my mom had with my father was an on and off relationship from which two children were born. In remembering him, my mom gave me the story no one in the family knew but her; even then, she told it with eyes filled with tears and under the appearance of much duress.

"I thought things would have been over between us after his wife threatened him about your brother the first time: 'If you see Lila again, I'll kill you.' I did not believe her. Neither did your father. But he just could not keep you to himself. He was a wonderful man and a wonderful father, not just to you and your brother but to all my kids. Every time he would come by the house, he did not have a toy just for you and your brother but he would have toys for all my kids: you, your brother, Ricky, and Weasel. Weasel would see him coming down the street (he parked his taxicab a little way down the road), and Weasel would be the first one to spot your daddy."

Momma was smiling now, as she would remember him and telling me her story. "That boy, Weasel, would run down the street and leap into your daddy's arms. Your daddy would catch him every time. He would have an arm full of groceries, but he would still catch him. When he would come by the house, he would bring food for the evening and groceries for the next couple of days. He was not just daddy to you and your brother. He was daddy to all my kids. Even though he was not their father, he was the only father they knew, and they loved him just the same."

Momma's face turned sorrowful as she continued talking about Daddy. "I did not know he had planned to tell his wife about you. If he would have told me, if he would have talked about it with me, I would have told him to keep silent. But when your father convinced himself of doing something, nobody could stop him."

Momma hung her head and said, "I still could not believe it. When I got word that your father had been killed, it was as if everything within me shut down. I sat down before I fell down. I looked at the guy, one of his friends, as he was telling me what had happened. I just looked at him and said, 'What did you say?' I must have been in shock. I could not believe what this man was telling me. He said, 'He's dead, Lila. He's gone.'"

As she was talking with me, sharing her heart about a story that she never talked about with anyone, Momma was shaking her head. I thought to myself, after all these years, *it still affects her*.

She said, "How… when… what happened? He said, 'His wife…' He paused and shook his head. 'His wife shot him dead while he was eating his breakfast.' 'But why?' I asked." Stinging tears began to fill my eyes, the kind of tears that hurt to cry because they do more stinging to your eyes than pouring water from your eyes.

As I continued to watch her, I could tell it was difficult for her to talk about this, and I could see that she was experiencing labored breathing as she continued to tell me the story no one else could share with me. She continued, "I kept asking him why? Why would she do such a thing? He finally said, 'What no one ever wanted to say out loud. Because, Lila, because he told his wife about the new baby. He told his wife about the new baby, and she shot him dead.'"

The new baby was me. At less than 3 months of age, I lost my father. He had been shot dead by his wife after having an on and off affair with my mom and impregnating her with my mom's second and fourth child, me.

Unfortunately, the day I lost my father, I also lost a significant part of my mother. Momma grew up in the District of Columbia. At the tender age of 12, she found herself pregnant with my oldest brother. I believe my mom grew up in a household where hard work was prominent, but affection was absent. Due to her pregnancy, mom left school in the 6th grade. There was no family member in another state or city that she could go to in order to keep the pregnancy hidden.

My mom was the oldest of my grandmother's children. While she was pregnant, she was given the responsibility to watch over, cook, and clean for her siblings while my grandmother worked as a maid in Georgetown. My grandmother had 16 children. Of the 16 children, 8 were 4 sets of twins. Only one set lived to be adults, and to date, only one of that set is living – my uncle. My mom had a lot of siblings to care for; however, after the birth of her first baby, Momma set out to take care of him, leaving him with one of her sisters to babysit as she worked whatever job she could find to feed and clothe him. Momma would later return to complete her high school diploma; however, she easily became a prime target to learn life the hard way, by trial and error.

Momma never married and had two more children after I was born. With a total of six children in her quiver, her absent father became apparent in her life and very real to me in my adult years. The signs of love, discipline, and care as a young girl were not warmly felt in my home nor environment. I did not know to look for such things, but the things my mom did and said to me as I was growing up showed me that she did love me; she loved me the best way she knew how. I suspect now that it was the same thing from her end as well with my grandmother; she went through the same thing with her mom and her absent father. Grandmother loved momma, but I could tell, she did not know how to love her. She loved Momma the best way she knew how.

This is what I mean by that. Many years ago, when my daughter was in grade school, she became friends with a girl at the Before & After Home Healthcare in our neighborhood where they would go to before and after school. I had met the girl's mom but did not know where she lived nor the environment in which she was raised. As it turned out, she asked my daughter to come to her "sleepover." The fact is, all I knew of the little girl was that she shared the space with my daughter in the Before & After care facility. I told my daughter that I was not letting her go to a sleepover where I had not met both parents nor did I know the environment in which they raised their kids. She fought me tooth and nail and even turned on the tears and the silent treatment. As this was a training ground for me, I did not know what to do.

Thank God for the Holy Spirit! This was a time that I was (as I am now) sold out to Christ. The Holy Spirit began to speak to me, and these were His words: *"It's best to listen to her cry now for hearing your NO than for you to see her tears after what will come later."* Beloved, I knew this was Holy Spirit because I was not smart enough to make up something so profound. When I got home after the crying and silence in the car, the woman who ran the Before & After care facility called me on my home phone and she said to me: "Lisa, I could not say anything to you because both you and the young girl's mother were present, but I'm glad that you said no to your daughter. Let me tell you why. They have drinking and card parties in that house 24/7 and should anything have happened to your daughter, it would be too late to take back what had been done." Wow! The Holy Spirit knows!

This is what I mean by loving someone and knowing how to love them, especially with being a parent. You have to love your children and love them to the point that you discipline them (past their rejection of you), say no and mean it, and teach them not only by what you say but more importantly by what you do. You have to love them to lead them, guide them, and be the directing point in their life. I believe my mom wanted to be able to do this and be the directing point in the lives of her children; unfortunately, due to her upbringing, she was limited in doing so. However, she did the best that she could, and for that I love her dearly and respect her.

I am sure there were times in her life when I believe she wanted to say no and she did; however, there were other times when life had beaten her down. With raising six children alone in the 1960s, working hard as a Black woman, trying to feed, clothe, and educate your children, and dealing with health and other issues, you get tired. She was tired. I believe she desired to say no, sometimes she screamed no – even through her tears. I still hear her "no's" now. Often times I would say, "Momma, why?" She would say, "Because I said so." I did not understand those "because I said so no's" then, but I do now.

The ups, the downs, the emotional difficulties, and the overall hardships she suffered, those which were visible and especially those which were not visible to me, were so very overwhelming to her during such tumultuous times. I have three children including one that was raised by his father's parents (I'll go in more detail in a later chapter) but raising two children alone in the 1990s was extremely difficult for me. I can only imagine what my mom went through. One thing is for sure, parenting alone can be quite challenging, hard, unfair, and overwhelming. Many women and men have done it, some successfully and others not as successfully. Although my young adult children are for the most part living life on their own terms with their own family and friends, I now see the fruit of some of my "no's" and some of my "yes's." Some of it is to be celebrated and some of it is to be received as doing the best that I could. As I was sharing with my daughter on her visit home in April 2021, I told her that if I had the chance to, I would <u>not</u> do anything different. I would let everything be as it has happened. In it happening as it did, I learned to love God my Savior, and in loving Him, I came to love myself. In loving myself, I came to love, respect, cherish, and appreciate each and every one of my children and my grandchildren in all of their personalities, just as they are, not for who I wish they would be or who I wish they would become, but for who they are and who they're growing to be.

Later in life, Momma received Christ during her senior years and was able to provide love in a precious and nurturing way. Her saying "no" to us in her later years was without any pushback. No questions asked at all. She said no, and she meant it. We, too, had learned the hard way that when Momma said "no," there was no need for questions. We simply did what was right or we did not. Either way, the lessons were ours to learn. She had showed the way, as best she knew how, and ours was now to take what she had given and apply it to our lives going forward.

Momma is now sleeping in Jesus. We sang her into the Kingdom of God as she took her last breath after breathing eight times. My family and many cherished, dear friends sang her into the arms of Jesus. She is now a part of the great cloud of witnesses the book of Hebrews speaks of: *"Therefore we also, since we are surrounded by so great a cloud of witnesses, let us lay aside every weight, and the sin which so easily ensnares us, and let us run with endurance the race that is set before us, looking unto Jesus, the author and finisher of our faith, who for the joy that was set before Him endured the cross, despising the shame, and has sat down at the right hand of the throne of God"* (Hebrews 12:1-2, NKJV).

Spoken Word

It seems as though I was traveling through a long but small tunnel
I saw a light at the end of the tunnel
I was in a hurry to get to the light
I felt the darkness behind me
Yes, I was in a hurry to get to the light
I heard voices which were surrounded by the light
One voice was welcoming, loving, and embracing
That voice must belong to my daddy, I thought
I hear my mommy; I feel her breathing
As I get closer to the light, I feel my mommy breathing
As I get closer to the light, I hear the voice beyond the light
Is that you, Daddy? I'm getting closer to you
I'm getting closer to the light
With one last push, I went from feeling my mommy breathing to
hearing my mommy breathe
I no longer saw darkness
I'm out in the light with wide eyes, looking, searching
screaming, Daddy, where are you?
Was that your voice I heard, Daddy?
Mommy, looking at me smiling
Mommy holding me close to her bosom
I'm screaming through words that are unrecognizable
Daddy, where are you?

Layer Two ~ Father to the Fatherless

Fatherless. The word itself seems empty, alone, and deserted. Yet, that is not how God desired nor intended life to be. The role of the father in the home and in the lives of his children is critically important. The lack of the presence and love of the father is detrimental to the emotional growth and development of his children. Without the father children survive, but that survival often times take on forms where the children simply exist and not thrive. No child should be placed in a situation or circumstance where they simply exist. With the love, care, guidance, affirmation, discipline, and direction of a father, a child has the ability to soar in life, academically, emotionally, psychologically, relationally, and definitely spiritually. However, without the love and care of a father, a child can feel left to the elements of life to simply get along. Of course, some children grow up and exceed these circumstances, but the missing element of the love and touch of a father is always sought out by the child.

We all know the meaning of the word fatherless as having no father because he is deceased or absent from the home. Yet, being fatherless looks different for so many children who grew up with this challenge. It can be a dad that is in prison, a dad that was killed, a dad that left his child and the mother and moved in with another woman and her kids, or a dad that married or remarried someone else. It could also be that the dad desired to explore his sexuality in an alternative lifestyle, such as a homosexual or as a full gender change into a woman. It is my personal experience that the child who grows up without ever hearing the sound of their father's voice, not seeing his face, not hearing his laughter, not seeing the color of his eyes, nor ever feeling his skin touch theirs brings about an ache in their heart, a longing that without their father's presence can almost never be relieved.

Yet God, the creator of the universe, created the role of fathers. Fathers, when they are operating within their role in a healthy fashion, possess a God-given authority. The father operates in his authority from a place of love, concern, compassion, and security over his children and his family. God designed the father to be the pillar, the stabilizing component of the family, who disciplines, leads, guides, affirms, strengthens, and provides for his family. God designed the mother to nurture the father's discipline, nurture the father's leading, nurture the father's guiding, nurture the father's affirmation, and nurture the father's ability to strengthen their child/children. Fathers present a masculine role to their children and often define the male figure that every young boy desires to emulate and the picture of the man who the young girl, his daughter, will grow to love and receive as her husband. However, if there is no male presence, then the young boy wanders in search of a "father figure" to gain direction, guidance, and especially affirmation and more importantly discipline. The same with the young girl. She searches and searches, often to the detriment of several relationships, soul-ties, marriage, and often times, unfortunately, divorce.

I believe we all can agree that fathers play a vital role in the family dynamics and the mental, emotional and spiritual growth and development of his children. In fact, according to the U.S. Department of Health and Human Services Administration for Children and Families, the Child Abuse and Neglect User Manual Series "The Importance of Fathers in the Healthy Development of Children"[1] provides a startling overview that we know to be true:

---

[1] Child Welfare Information Gateway. 2006. "The Importance of Fathers in the Healthy Development of Children." Washington, DC: U.S. Department of Health and Human Services, Children's Bureau.

"The Impact of the Mother-Father Relationship on Child Outcomes"

"Fathers have a direct impact on the well-being of their children. Fathers influence their children in large part through the quality of their relationship with the mother of their children. A father who has a good relationship with the mother of their children is more likely to be involved and to spend time with the children and to have children who are psychologically and emotionally healthier."

"The Impact of Fathers on Cognitive Ability and Educational Achievement"

"Children with involved, caring fathers have better educational outcomes."

"The Impact of Fathers on Psychological Well-Being and Social Behavior"

"Even from birth, children who have an involved father are more likely to be emotionally secure, be confident to explore their surroundings, and, as they grow older have better social connections with peers."

Fathers are and should be the stabilizing component of every family. The work of the father can never be completed by the mother, nor was it meant to be. The roles of father and mother were meant to function, dominate, rule, and teach their children to do so **together**. However, when a woman is placed in a situation where she is to act as mother and father, both she and the children suffer. Nor was the father meant to be the only parent in the home; such a situation presents an unbalanced unit of the ordained desire of God, in which the role of both husband and wife, male and female, made in the image and likeness of God, take authority and procreate as instructed by God. With this understanding, neither father nor mother were ever meant to act within both roles singularly, but we often find this to be the case.

Growing up without a father in my young eyes, young heart, and young mind was quite difficult. God was gracious to me during those times, because most of the kids in the apartments and in the neighborhoods where I lived as a young girl were quite familiar with this scenario. In fact, recalling the area where I grew up as a young child, there were few families where the father or father figure was "occasionally" present.

I remember there were six apartment buildings in this particular apartment complex. Most apartment buildings had four floors with four apartment homes located on each floor; other apartment buildings had five floors which included basement apartments. This stands out to me now in recalling this situation because out of all the apartment buildings and all of the families living in these apartments, I knew most if not all of the school-aged children, because I went to school with them as well as other neighborhood youngsters from kindergarten to 6th grade. Some I grew quite close to as children sometimes would, and others were simply school/classroom friends. I mention this scenario because throughout the time of my living in the apartment complex, I do not recall seeing a family move in and stay together throughout my time there before we moved to another location. I lived in that apartment complex for more than 6 years, and throughout that time, the fathers that were part of a family were few and far in between.

I do recall only one family that remained close to our family, even to this present day. A young man who is the oldest son of this divorced family lived in the apartment complex and became best friends to my brother, and they are still friends to this day. He is currently in the ministry, and occasionally we have the opportunity to connect with one another. I bring this family's story up because their family was the only family within the apartment complex where the father, although divorced from the mother and not living in the home, remained a steady part of the children's lives. The father was a businessman and operated a radio/dancing studio out of the Baltimore area and used to be on TV. Occasionally, all the neighborhood kids, myself included, would gather around a neighbor's TV to watch this show and see the father, who was the announcer on the show. On a bi-weekly or monthly basis, he would be in the neighborhood visiting his kids. We would see him on TV every Saturday night, and we would see him visiting his children. It was very impressionable on me because out of all the apartments in the apartment complex, this was the only family, the only father, with whom I saw this consistency.

I recognize that the struggle during times of slavery was to separate families so that the bond of family and unity were severed. Fathers were sold to slave owners who travelled from one part of the country, paid for the father, broke up the family and returned to their home in another part of the country. This set up repeated itself with the mother and often times with the children as well, separating them from one another. However, the idea of both the enemy of our souls and the slave-master who brought and purchased the slaves was to remove the father, the stabilizing, solidifying force of the family unit, from the family. This system set up an engrained, disruptive, and debilitating heritage that we still see in place today among our black families. Unfortunately, it is no longer the slave-master in the form of a white male who is removing the father from the family. Now, it is the "system" which was birthed through the mindset of slavery and the slave-master that "sets up" the fathers to leave the mothers with child or children in tow with the false thinking that she will make it; everyone else did before her, and she will, too.

Again, this separation of fathers from mothers and children, this separation of the family, was never God's plan for humanity. This was never God's plan for the black community, the white community, the red, nor the tan or brown community. This was never God's plan for humanity. God's plan is very clear, and it remains His plan to this day. Genesis 1:27-28 (NKJV) says, *"So God created man in His own image; in the image of God He created him; male and female He created them. Then God blessed them, and God said to them, 'Be fruitful and multiply; fill the earth and subdue it; have dominion over the fish of the sea, over the birds of the air, and over every living thing that moves on the earth.'"*

Many fathers are no longer in the home due to divorce, marital separation, never being married, an ongoing on-and-off relationship with the mother of their child/children, prison, or drug and/or alcoholic addictions that have placed them away from their families. Some fathers are outside of the home due to military duty, business travel which requires being away from the home for large amounts of time, or unfortunately death. It is imperative that first and foremost, we understand God's heart and come away from our own understandings, perceptions, and the ways in which we have seen the family dynamic lived out in the past or present. God intended that the family be united in prayer, grow together in love to endure hardship, and stay together. Unfortunately, with humanity endeavoring to do things their way, both male and female, we have made shipwrecks of our families and have walked away from a wonderful bond that could have, through Christ, been strengthened to last a life time.

Beloved, I say to you, God created family. I write for you Genesis 2:7-8 and 15-24 (NKJV): *⁷ And the LORD God formed man of the dust of the ground, and breathed into his nostrils the breath of life; and man became a living being. ⁸ The LORD God planted a garden eastward in Eden, and there He put the man whom He had formed.* **And**, *¹⁵ Then the LORD God took the man and put him in the garden of Eden to tend and keep it. ¹⁶ And the LORD God commanded the man, saying, "Of every tree of the garden you may freely eat; ¹⁷ but of the tree of the knowledge of good and evil you shall not eat, for in the day that you eat of it you shall surely die." ¹⁸ And the LORD God said, "It is not good that man should be alone; I will make him a helper comparable to him." ¹⁹ Out of the ground the LORD God formed every beast of the field and every bird of the air, and brought them to Adam to see what he would call them. And whatever Adam called each living creature, that was its name. ²⁰ So Adam gave names to all cattle, to the birds of the air, and to every beast of the field. But for Adam there was not found a helper* *comparable to him. ²¹ And the* LORD *God caused a deep sleep to fall on Adam, and he slept; and He took one of his ribs, and closed up the flesh in its place. ²² Then the rib which the* LORD *God had taken from man He made into a woman, and He brought her to the man. ²³ And Adam said: "This is now bone of my bones and flesh of my flesh; She shall be called Woman, Because she was taken out of Man."*

I draw your attention to the last phrase of verse 24 ("This is now bone of my bones and flesh of my flesh"); at this beautiful moment, unity was created. Adam acknowledged his woman, given to him by God. His woman was a helper who complemented him in every way. Even once sin entered their environment and thereafter, they remained complementary to one another. One of the most beautiful ways that the woman complemented the man was in procreation. She received his seed which fertilized her egg, and she nurtured and held this beautiful being in her womb until it was time to give birth. At the time of birthing, the woman brought forth a child which complemented not only the man but also the woman as the child is the offspring of both.

The unity of the family remains in the earth to this day and throughout time continues to be tested and challenged. Yet what God created remains: man, woman, mother, father, the heavens, the sun, the moon, the stars and the earth in all of their beauty and yes, the family. That which God created remains in the earth no matter the challenge. They all still remain, and it is all still good!

Father to the Fatherless

Psalm 68:5

To the fatherless, He is a Father.
To the widow, He is a champion friend.
To the lonely, He makes them part of a family.
To the prisoners, He leads into prosperity until they sing for joy.
This is our Holy God in His Holy Place!
But for the rebels there is heartache and despair.

My search for my dad did not begin as an older woman, as I am now. No, my search for my dad began as a young girl as I was told bits and pieces of the story of his death. It was not until my mom told me the whole story much later in life, with pain and even tears in her eyes flowing from her heart, that I finally understood and appreciated her silence during my younger years.

Yet, my heart has longed for, even yearned for, the kind of relationship that women, toddlers, young girls, teenage girls, young women, and maybe even older women experience as they walk and talk with their fathers. How does it feel to experience the weight of the father's arms lifting you to safety? From the bed at night where you wet yourself, and the place where you slept was no longer comfortable but wet and stinging your legs and your bottom, your cry in the middle of the night was met with your mother and occasionally by your dad; I've never felt that. How was the touch of his fingers as I curled my tiny hands around his finger or thumb? Were my father's hands the hands of a skilled worker, bruised by the occasional nail and hammer, or were they the hands of a father carrying a briefcase to the next meeting? In my mind's eye, I see him lifting me up as I lift my hands to him with the look in my eyes, even before the words come to my mouth, "Daddy, pick me up." He would pick me up, taking both his hands and placing them under my arms, lifting me up, all the while never taking his eyes off me, like a driver turning the wheel, eyes peeled in the direction of the turn. He was looking at me, and I was looking at him, until I am finally close to him, face to face. In my imagination, I am listening to him breathe, listening and feeling every step he takes as he carries me in his arms for even the shortest of time.

As I was told, my daddy was a taxicab driver. But I've often wondered, what does my daddy's voice sound like? I imagine him looking at me, smiling; bringing his nose close to my face to touch my skin. I feel the briskness of his beard as he comes close and I smile, I laugh because his beard tickles me. He thinks it is his hands tickling me. "No, Daddy, it's your beard tickling my skin. Your beard bristling up around my neck as you bury your face into my neck and collar bones, mumbling, 'What's wrong with my snookum?'"

I have never seen my daddy, neither in form nor in picture. To the best of my recollection, I do not remember his eyes meeting mine, although I wish I did. I do not remember feeling the touch of his skin, although I wish I did. I do not know what it felt like to feel his breath close on me after lifting me up or blowing pretend bubbles in my face as adults do with babies to garner a laugh at the tinkle of their nose or the sudden burst of air in their baby's eyes. Again, I wish I did. I do not recall the sound of my father's voice. However, my heart longs for this the most: I have often wondered what nickname he would have called me, if any.

During times when I'm looking up at the dark starry sky, I wonder to myself, how did my daddy smell? In those days, during the sixties, men would wear Aqua Velva, English Leather, Old Spice, or even Brut aftershave; I wonder which one my daddy wore, if any. I do not remember any sentiments, neither happy nor sad; if I had just one, I could carry that with me to my grave. But I'm hoping to see him on the other side of life and experience his smile, the brightness of his eyes, and his laughter once he sees me, taking hold of his hands and walking with him in Heaven's gardens, if he made the Lord his savior before his life was taken from him.

The one thing I do have of my father, besides his DNA, is his last name. He gave me his last name, Pate. I may have his eyes or his hair line. I don't know, really. I may have my daddy's ears, nose, or even his smile; I don't know really. But one thing is for sure that I do know, I have his last name. My mom once told me, "Your daddy was a 'giving man.'" For me, that explains a lot and reveals to me a lot about the way I am. I, too, am a giving person; but to be fair, my mom was also a giver. She would give her coat to a person who had none in the dead of winter. I often wondered what other inner characteristics I may have inherited from my father that I am not aware of. One thing I have come to realize over time, especially as an adult woman, was that my father stood up for truth, even in the midst of his own wrong, which was detrimental to his marriage and proved to be deathly to his own life. He stood up for truth. I was his truth, and he would not deny me, even under the penalty of death. Now, to be honest and fair, I wish he would have honored the truth of his marriage and had not entered into a relationship with my mom, nor any other woman for that matter, but that would have prevented me from being born.

God Has a Plan – Choose His Plan for You

Yet in me not knowing my daddy, I have discovered a love in my heavenly Father that I have not known in my earthly father. I look to my heavenly Father whom I have grown to love, cherish, trust, and depend on as though my life depends upon it, because both now and eternally, it does. I have learned that God watches over our lives and has plans and purposes for us, but in order for those plans and purposes to be carried out for His Glory and fulfillment, I believe that we must be connected to Him.

The Word of God says in Jeremiah 29:11 (NKJV), *"For I know the thoughts that I think toward you, says the LORD, thoughts of peace and not of evil, to give you a future and a hope."* It is beautiful and refreshing to read in the Word of God that He has thoughts about you and me. This particular Scripture was written during a time when the Israelite nation was being punished by God and were subjected to 70 years of Babylon enslavement. Yet God says to them in a very loving manner, even in the midst of telling them that they would be enslaved by a people that they hated and who hated them as well, *"I know the thoughts that I think toward you…"* Even after we have lived out our lives in lifestyles that would not honor our parents, family, nor God, God still says to us: *I know the thoughts that I think toward you…* God thinks thoughts towards you and me – thoughts of peace and not of evil, to give us a hope and a future. Even after my life of prostitution, even after my life of homelessness, even after my life of fatherlessness, even after my rebellion, even after my shame, even after my rejection, even after all of my guilt, even after _____ (*you fill in the blank for yourself*). God knows the thoughts He thinks towards you and me, thoughts of good and not evil, thoughts to give us a hope and a future. God still thinks thoughts about you – good thoughts to prosper you and that would lead you to an expected end.

    The one thing that God will never do is force His will on anyone. He did not do it in the Garden of Eden, and He will not do it here in this current age. What makes the human race made in the image of God so very much like our Creator is that we all have a will. We do not walk as animals, nor operate as animals do. We are made in the image of our Creator God, and we are made with the mindset of our own free wills. Genesis 1:26-27 (NLT) says, *"Then God said, 'Let us make human beings in our image, to be like us. They will reign over the fish in the sea, the birds in the sky, the livestock, all the wild animals on the earth, and the small animals that scurry along the ground.' So God created human beings in his own image. In the image of God he created them; male and female he created them."*

    Because we have our own free will, we can choose what we will do and who we will serve. Joshua 24:15 (NLT, emphasis mine) says, *"But if you refuse to serve the LORD,* **then choose today whom you will serve***. Would you prefer the gods your ancestors served* *beyond the Euphrates? Or will it be the gods of the Amorites in whose land you now live? But as for me and my family, we will serve the LORD."* We can choose who we will surrender our lives to – either to sin, shame, death, and destruction or to life and eternity. It is as simple as that. It is not complicated at all.

Submitting to God's Plan

When you and I submit our lives to God, we choose God, our Heavenly Father, and ask Him to be Lord in and over our lives. When He comes into our hearts, takes His rightful place upon the throne of our hearts, and moves us and our idols (people, places, things, money, flesh, etc.) off of the throne of our hearts, things in our lives begin to change. As we read His Word and it begins to renew our minds, our spirits are refreshed and renewed by the washing of the Word of God (Ephesians 5:26) and our hearts are renewed to the life that Christ desires for us to live in Him (Ezekiel 36:26). Our hearts are changed from the old things that used to come from our heart such as sin, which took the form of rebellion, resentment, anger, bitterness, depression, shame, unforgiveness, and the like.

According to Jeremiah 24:7 (NKJV): *"Then I will give them a heart to know Me, that I am the Lord; and they shall be My people, and I will be their God, for they shall return to Me with their whole heart."* When our minds are renewed and our hearts are changed by the Word of God, our lives are changed for the better. We see things differently. We no longer look at things from the eyes of a defeated, woe is me, I have nothing, and I am not worth anything mentality **to** I am the righteousness of God in Christ Jesus and I am above only and never beneath (2 Corinthians 5:21 and Deuteronomy 28:13).

But please realize, this is a process as no person being born of a woman is born as an adult. We are all born as infants. Over the process of time, we grow into toddlers, adolescents, tweens, teens, young adults, adults, and finally seniors. You have to actually receive (read/intake) and believe the Word of God, and your walk and lifestyle can continuously change to exemplify your belief in Christ and His Word. You no longer have the perspective of trying as hard as you can to live holy or "white knuckle it" as described by my former senior pastor and friend, Bishop James R. Izzard, Jr., but it flows from your heart. What does not "flow," the Word of God identifies and addresses it. With time and patience in the presence of the Lord, the Holy Spirit deals with the issue *with* you and helps you to identify it, admit it, confess it, overcome it, and live victorious over it (Romans 6:12-14).

People Pleasing Never Pleases People

I have learned to look to the pleasing eye and affirming heart of my heavenly Father. I admit that most of the trouble that I continued to strive with in my heart was looking to the appealing eyes of man. Do you know and realize that you can never please man? I did not know this until I was well past my 40s. I was extremely hard-headed and stubborn, even towards the Holy Spirit. I kept believing and acting with my **works**. I sincerely and whole-heartedly believed that once people saw how hard I worked and how much I sacrificed, they would love me; if they did not love me, they would at least have to like me. This people pleasing is one of the pillar foundations for the spirit of rejection. Well at the end of the day, the people I was trying so desperately to please did not like me nor respect me. I had to learn that my works, even if they were for them, would never please them. This was a very hard lesson for me to learn, as I am sure it is for some of you. The lesson I had to learn, under extreme and great difficulty, was that people pleasing never pleases people. ***People pleasing never pleases people***. Only when you seek to please the "audience of One" (the Lord) will your works, labors of love, and acts of kindness and service for Him truly be appreciated and rewarded.

These are just a few of the lessons that a loving Father, my Heavenly Father, had to teach me in the crucibles of life, *when I was ready to learn them*. But I could not learn them until He truly became Lord in my life, I accepted Him as my Heavenly Father, and I stopped trying to make ways for myself. I had to learn that by my Heavenly Father adopting me into the royal family, I was no longer the person who was cast out, alone, separated by my life, actions, and choices, and unworthy to be received and loved. My Heavenly Father, through the washing of His Word in and over my heart and my life, I had to continuously recognize, receive, and walk in the fact, the truth of His Word, that I was no longer an orphan.

An orphan feels out of place, rejected, alone, separated, and unworthy, to say the least. This is how I felt being fatherless, and thus I was continuously working to receive validation and be affirmed, accepted, and allowed "admittance" into friendships, special groups in the church, cliques, invites to the parties that I had heard about after the event took place, and someone willing to sit next to me. There were so many times that I would want to scream saying, "Thank you, thank you so very much for sitting next to me!" to the person who had come to sit next to me during the church's leadership meetings. I often restrained myself from doing so, realizing that I did not want to appear foolish, although I certainly felt foolish. Truly, this perverted perception of mine and the deception of the enemy had nothing to do with the church nor the leaders. **This was the enemy's deception working on and in my mind**. But when you are or you see yourself as an orphan, this is how you act; this is your continued response to life. This is how you feel, and often times, this is how you **reply in life and about life** out of your brokenness. You respond out of this rejected place.

Receive Christ and Move on to Freedom in Christ

Receiving Christ, the Son of God, as Lord and God the Father as my Heavenly Father changed all of that for me after many, many years. I was not "upgraded." I did not level up, neither did I "pivot."

However, I was grafted into the Family of God and emerged into the waters of the Baptism of the Holy Spirit. Ephesians 1:5 (NLT) says, *"God decided in advance to adopt us into his own family by bringing us to himself through Jesus Christ. This is what he wanted to do, and it gave him great pleasure."* The loving Father, through His Word and by His presence, encountered my heart. He visited, revisited, and revisited again every room in my heart and soul that I had quarantined off without even realizing it. The Holy Spirit began to meet with me in the intimacy of my heart and my mind and walk with me through my childhood, places where I had placed boundaries around and areas that I had left open doors that provided easy access to the enemy of my soul. Christ helped me to see and acknowledge what happened; through His love and forgiveness, He helped me to forgive myself for things I had absolutely no control over; circumstances, situations, and decisions that I had made and allowed to happen; and ***things that I had done that I was literally tormenting myself over, even into my adulthood***.

      The Holy Spirit provided and continues to provide even now the washing of the water through the Word of God, refreshing springs of forgiveness, admittance, and acceptance from things that I used to allow to torment me and hold me back from moving forward, thinking forward, talking forward, and reaching forward. I now move from room to room in my entire life, in my heart and in my mind, accepting and forgiving what happened, ***even if I caused it***, moving on to freedom, and stepping over into victory, because of Christ, who has redeemed me from it ALL! The price of my redemption was ETERNALLY PAID with the Blood of the Lamb of Jesus Christ, my Lord. I no longer hold onto old addresses (places where my mind used to go when feeling abandoned and rejected), old mindsets, old ways, old habits, old titles/names in my mind (ugly, buckteeth, baldheaded, skinny or fat, crackhead, whore, or prostitute), old names that folks called me behind my back or otherwise, or names that I answered to and names that I once called myself. My Heavenly Father calls me by the ultimate name, HIS. He calls me His Daughter, His Beloved, and

His Child. Ephesians 1:11-14 (NKJV) says: *"¹¹ In Him also we have obtained an inheritance, being predestined according to the purpose of Him who works all things according to the counsel of His will, ¹² that we who first trusted in Christ should be to the praise of His glory. ¹³ In Him you also trusted, after you heard the word of truth, the gospel of your salvation; in whom also, having believed, you were sealed with the Holy Spirit of promise, ¹⁴ who is the guarantee of our inheritance until the redemption of the purchased possession, to the praise of His glory."*

Layer Three ~ Delayed Growth

The importance of a father's presence and his role in the life of a child is critical. The absence of a loving and involved father and the role he plays, in support of the mother as well as the children, provides emotional, psychological, educational, and developmental growth to be experienced and affirmation received by the child/children. Unfortunately, when this role is absent from the home, the effects grow and expand throughout the child's life, especially if the role of the father in some form is not made available to the child/children. For me, the absence of the love of my father was crucial, even critical, in my life.

Many scholarly articles address the fact that the significance of a father's involvement in the development of the child/children can determine the child's/children's emotional, psychological and academic development as well as the basic well-being within the family unit. "On the other hand, what is especially promising with the effects of father engagement is that it seems to differentially influence desirable outcomes."[2] According to Apostle John Eckhardt, in his book *Destroying the Spirit of Rejection*, "But there is no substitute for a committed father in the home."[3] It is important to realize that "Develop-mentally, children with involved fathers are also less likely to drop out of school, act out in school, and/or engage in risky

---

[2] A. Sarkadi, R. Kristiansson, F. Oberklaid, and S. Bremberg, "Fathers' Involvement and Children's Developmental Outcomes: A Systematic Review of Longitudinal Studies," *Acta Pædiatrica* 97 (2008): 157. **https://doi.org/10.1111/j.1651-2227.2007.00572.x**

[3] John Eckhardt, *Destroying the Spirit of Rejection* (Lake Mary, FL: Charisma House, 2006), [page 20].

behaviors in adolescence, thus highlighting the notable effect that a father can have on a child's academic well-being."[4] We must understand that there is an order God has established for the home that provides a defense against the enemy's attacks on our children. It is my experience that nothing can make up for a father's love being demonstrated for both a daughter and a son. I am viewing this difficulty both from the perspective of a daughter who grew up not knowing my father as well as being the parent of my son and daughter who grew up without a father in the home. This challenge has proven to be almost detrimental to me. The lack of my father's presence in our home and in my life was crucial for my emotional and psychological development and my self-awareness as a person, as a young girl, as a young lady, and even as a woman.

I admit that I did not truly become aware of myself as a woman and all of its actualization until extremely late in life, which is why this section is titled "Delayed Growth." My growth and the delays that I experienced (psychologically, emotionally, and academically) were not only due to the absence of my father and the absence of a father figure in the home but also due to predators in and outside of the home who preyed on vulnerable children such as myself. The hard fact is that most children who are subject to molestation, rape, and sexual abuse often are preyed upon because there was not a father nor a father figure in the home or in the life of the child. For me, this is where my trouble began.

At a young age, while I was in kindergarten, I was sexually molested by a family member. The person who molested me was the

---

[4] S. M. Ellis, Y. S. Khan, V. W. Harris, R. McWilliams, and D. Converse, "The Impact of Fathers on Children's Well-Being," *UF-IFAS Extension* (2014): 2. https://www.researchgate.net/profile/Victor-Harris-2/publication/270882185_The_Impact_of_Fathers_on_Children's_Well-Being_1/links/54b6ae120cf24eb34f6d5c2b/The-Impact-of-Fathers-on-Childrens-Well-Being-1.pdf

very same person who taught me the alphabet, numbers, and how to read, write, and count. This behavior created an inability to recognize right from wrong within me. I felt that what was being done to me was wrong, but because it was practiced along with the things that were normal, I was unable to differentiate and determine that this was wrong, especially still being a child. The abuser himself was received by me, even though the abuse itself was acted out under perverted and malicious coercion. Unfortunately, I did not recognize it as wrong; I was too young to recognize such behavior. Because this person who manipulated my innocence was trusted by me and my family, I based the shame and the wrongdoing in my heart and within my conscience. Over time, they simply ate away at me and my inability to believe and trust that what I was feeling and thinking were wrong. Over time, these feelings were not spoken of nor identified, and they dulled my feelings and my senses. They brought about a second personality of sorts that I have deemed undeniably second guessing myself. How could I know or be sure what was happening to me was wrong? Therefore, I must be wrong, and they must be right.

    This molestation did not initially begin with penetration; it began with whispering, touching, and exposing my ears and eyes to things a child should never see, hear, or even be aware of. But because the individual masked their behavior with and under the innocence of schoolwork, helping me, and pretending to care for me and my family, my innocence was stolen right from under my family's eyes. I do not blame my family, nor do I blame my mom who was the head of our household. I do not excuse any wrongdoing; however, I will say this: my mom did the best she knew how to do. She was not aware of what was going on, and I will not know her heart fully until we both are in Glory and by that time, seeing Christ and our glorified bodies, it will not be a priority. I have forgiven the person and have also forgiven myself. To the extent that I believe that I needed to, I have forgiven my mom.

    I go in depth regarding this to help someone else get free if this kind of behavior in their life has also led them to drug abuse, silent and tormenting thoughts, self-hatred, cutting themselves, and any or all abuse in any form. Friend, freedom is available in Christ! I had to discover true freedom in Him, and so can you.

Due to the sexual molestation and physical abuse, I began acting and showing out in class at school, which manifested as me yelling at teachers and anyone in authority, screaming and fighting other children, not completing the schoolwork nor homework, total rebellion, and utter disobedience. Although I was alert in class, I was alert for all of the wrong reasons because I was not paying attention. Inwardly, I was crying out, but I did not know what I was crying out for nor why I was crying and acting out. Instead, I acted out in displays of anger, disrupting everything and everyone, everywhere I went. Remember the cartoon character of the Tasmanian Devil? Wherever he would go, he would spin wildly out of control and a discombobulated or confused atmosphere was a result of his presence. That was me in elementary school, though not junior high nor high school.

I became known for the trouble that surrounded me. I was confused. Peacefulness and calmness escaped my mind and my heart. I learned not to rely on, believe in, nor trust in those who were in authority; in my mind, the person who was in authority (at least over me) was molesting me. I soon believed that everyone, especially those in authority, could or would eventually misuse me. This was such a lonely place in my life. As I continued to grow from my early classes in elementary school, unfortunately I, too, became the abuser. As I was abused and thought the actions performed on and towards me were normal, I began to act out and hurt people around me; again, I thought my actions were normal. It is not my story to tell, but I have confessed my wrong and sought forgiveness from the individuals I have hurt. It is not my heart to make things seem like I was the only person wronged; however, it is very true that hurt people hurt people.

I began as young girl cursing, swearing, and speaking, saying, and thinking hateful words that I heard other adults and other kids say to me. These actions and behaviors framed my young life and my young world. Unfortunately, because they continued in one form or another throughout my childhood and well into my young adulthood, they framed my perception of myself. There were times I was called the "B" word by adults who had authority over me while I was just a child. I did not even know what the word meant, though I knew it was not a pretty word and it felt demeaning. As an adult typing these words now, I remember those feelings.

As I continued to grow and develop as a young girl, I was emotionally distraught to the point that mental adjustments I should have been able to process and make from a healthy perspective were not within my reach. I was not able to identify wrong or incorrect thinking. I thought and actually believed that what I was going through was normal; not that it was right, good, or bad but that it was normal because it was all that I had known up until that present time. My emotional and psychological development and my educational growth were delayed as a young child and later as a teenager. My cognizant awareness was hanging in the balance, but God intervened and turned this around.

The enemy opened the door of abuse and molestation in my life as a child. These forms of mistreatment developed an inability to trust people within my psyche, especially boys and men; however, girls and women soon followed suit in my distrust. I felt that I could not trust any adults. All of the adults in my life at that time (teachers, neighbors, family friends, and even my mom) responded to my actions of disruption and outright disobedience with anger. They were angry, and I was angry. I was also confused, sad, and quite frankly a very bad and emotionally fragmented child. I acted out constantly. The root cause as to why I was acting out appeared to escape everyone. But it never escaped God!

We often do not realize it until later on in life, but the enemy was exposing me, even as a child, to destructive methods and habits. I will go further in detail about unhealthy exposure in the next chapter. That is one of the greatest tricks of the enemy: exposure, especially at an early age. The enemy exposes people to situations, feelings, and desires, especially outside of the context of holiness and the truth of God's word, that would eventually drive us, compel us, swallow us whole, and render us lifeless or useless in life. With the exposure, the enemy uses our eyes, ears, hands, mind, thoughts, dreams, and anything else he can to begin his entrapment into a life-long habit of deranged and cynical dysfunction. For me, it was the molestation, but that was simply the beginning. Other areas of my life that were affected by this disruption in my childhood left me with the inability to connect with people without fear of them hurting, using, or abusing me. True development of my self-worth was affected as well as my self-esteem, and the meaning and articulation of healthy and safe boundaries. It also created fear of people, fear of trusting people, anger, angry outbursts, and the need to overcompensate and over-extend myself in dealing with people.

I have worked as a secretary for most of my adult life in law firms and medical offices. I once had an attorney who I was working for tell me, "You would work yourself to death or die trying, if I let you." I had to learn that I was doing that under the guise of an excellent work ethic. Having an excellent work ethic has nothing to do with working until you have lost yourself in the doing of the work. You end up valuing the work instead of your health, and you also teach others to value your work instead of your health in the process; what kind of ethic is that? There is a balance in doing an excellent job because you have done your absolute best. That is it, nothing more and nothing less.

I learned the hard way to stop sabotaging my own energy, my own desires, and my own dreams. I learned the very hard lesson of not giving up. The most difficult lesson for me was not quitting. I was not able to make the connection between the molestation and my quitting and giving up on myself. I would quit the absolute best jobs as soon as a little bit of trouble would rise up. I would quit people, friends, circumstances, and situations. I would mentally and emotionally check out, even though the circumstances and situations were still going on. It was not until many years later during a process of healing, a deep healing in my mind, emotions, soul, and spirit that the Holy Spirit began to delve into my history. He was well aware of my history, but prior to that time, I was unwilling to face and work through it. But over the process of time, the Holy Spirit continued to work with me, softening my heart until I became pliable in His hands. I also became submitted to Him as Lord in every area of my life.

With this acceptance in my heart, the Holy Spirit began asking me questions like, *"Why are you leaving? Why are you giving up on YOU? Why are you avoiding or procrastinating in this which My hands have assigned for you at this time? Did I not say in My Word that I would never leave you nor forsake you? If you believe My Word, why won't you truly believe Me and trust Me to be with you through this situation and/or circumstance?"* My answer was that I did not want to go through enduring the emotional hurt and the soul pain, not realizing that I was emotionally connecting the hurt and the pain of my childhood trauma and all that it entailed to the current painful situation or circumstance. When I would go through a difficult situation, I **would not** take it because my emotions and my soul were viewing it as the childhood trauma – not the actual trauma that I was facing at that time, but the emotional and/or mental pain that was associated with my childhood trauma. I was not able to distinguish or differentiate between the past trauma, the molestation and abuse of my childhood, and my physical response to the trauma that I was experiencing in the moment. My response was to quit – stop the action of what is taking place.

This prevented friendships from forming in my life, not because of the people themselves, but because of me. If something happened in the friendship (I am simply speaking on the level of girl to girl friendship), I would lose the friendship. I lost a lot of friends because I had an inability to trust; I was undeniably waiting for the moment when that person would say or do something that I would consider hurtful and that would be the "box checked" signal for me. They did it and I was out; I quit, and I left the friendship. I no longer wanted to be friends with them. But if the truth were being told, I was not really being a friend. I found out well into my forties that true friends may have relational ups and downs and husbands and wives have ups and downs; however, that does not constitute a reason for leaving and ending the friendship nor marriage. I had to learn that you do not give up on people, you do not give up on relationships, and you do not quit life, physically, mentally, or emotionally. You do not quit life, and you do not quit people, period.

I had to learn that things that happen in any kind of relationship do not mean that the persons involved could not be trusted. What it does mean is that this is an area that needs to be opened up and examined by two mature people to come together, talk the situation or circumstance through, find common ground, and move forward from there. I did not experience this open dialogue with people and adjusting my relational barometer until late in life, but I can now share with you that I am no longer quick to make fast judgements. I am also no longer quick to come to what I have coined as "rapid conclusions" where you sum a person up by what they did or did not do, how they acted or reacted, or how they responded or did not respond. I have learned to share grace over periods of time and to see people through the eyes of my Heavenly Father. The mistakes we make do not cancel us out as human beings, nor do they cancel us out as children of God, nor do they cancel out the right for friendship.

Am I saying that we have to accept everyone? No; we have to use wisdom. There is not peace nor wisdom in being around someone who has showed you who they truly are and who displays no desire to work on themselves to be friends with you. You cannot right every wrong in a person. I am not saying be gullible; however, your life as you grow and mature should become less about drama and more about you growing to live and experience life better. As I have begun to be even more self-aware and grow and mature as a person, as a woman, and as a woman of God, I no longer quit friends or cancel people out of my life. Let me be clear, I do not make you stay if you want to go. Our posture has to be one of not throwing people away nor quitting and giving up on ourselves due to unhealed traumas in our past.

Getting healed, dealing with my traumas, and allowing the Holy Spirit to begin to confront areas that I had buried deep under my emotional and mental stresses were severely difficult. It was not easy, but it was so very necessary! I could not stay 5 years old emotionally forever. I could not stay 10 years old emotionally forever. I could not stay 25 years old emotionally forever. I had to mature emotionally, physically, and psychologically. I could not remain in a place where I was emotionally, physically, psychologically, or even spiritually delayed due to childhood traumas. I could not remain in the infancy, childhood, tween, teenage, or young adult stages of life without having the Holy Spirit to bring about healing in my soul and in my spirit. This allowed me to move forward in my life, receive and walk in deliverance, and experience life abundantly and triumphantly in every area of my life. This took time; in fact, it took years, and it is still not completed. The Holy Spirit is still working in me, perfecting His perfect plan and purposes. It is important for you to know that this is not an instantaneous session, although the Lord can do so if He chooses to. However, often times, we want a quick work done because we do not want to go through the process of endurance during our healing journey.

The labor that you allow in and through your life by the Holy Spirit will provide for you instruction, guidance, wisdom, purpose, stability, and sustainability for yourself and others who may have the privilege of calling you friend. We ought not to rush when the Holy Spirit is doing His greatest work in our lives – working on us from the inside out. Honestly, we cannot rush it any way, but what we tend to do is leave the work site. We get busy and involve ourselves in other "ministry" and/or life-related matters and excuse our own selves from the work because we feel healed or because we seem okay. We may have even started smiling and completing our own sentences and we think, "Hey, I'm doing okay." Often times when the Holy Spirit is healing an area or some areas in our lives, be it childhood traumas, separation anxieties, anger issues, and/or rejection issues and syndromes, these deep rooted works take time, even secluded times away from the masses, with quiet one on one time in the Word of God and in the presence of the Holy Spirit. One of the most beautiful ways that I have experienced healing is through the process of time, learning lessons then failing at most lessons and retaking the test, one moment, one day, one week, one month and one year at a time.

The most precious deliverance I have received is when the Lord delivered me from crack cocaine. This Scripture rings true for me as the Word declares, *"Therefore if the Son makes you free, you shall be free indeed."* John 8:36 (NKJV). Although I have made mistakes and mishaps in other areas, drugs and cigarettes were not one of those "do overs" in my life. The Lord completely removed the taste and the desire from my heart and has given me a distinct hatred for both of those vices. After more than 33 years, I am still thanking Him! In fact, every time I drive by or run across a path of my former life, I become overwhelmed both with joy and thankfulness because I recognize it clearly. I still whisper, "God, thank you!" The blood of the Lord Jesus Christ has cleansed me and He has removed those severe vices from my life. As a testimony, I know that He can and given the opportunity, He desires to do the same and even more for you and everyone who comes to Him for such deliverance.

Do you recall the story of Jesus cleansing the leper? Read the following story from Luke chapter 5 slowly; perhaps see it with fresh eyes and gain additional insight from the Holy Spirit. Often I find that I have missed intricate details the Holy Spirit is pointing out to me. As Dr. Kenneth Hill (former senior pastor of Harvest Temple COG) would often say to us as his members, "You read the Scriptures too fast; slow down."

"And it happened when He was in a certain city, that behold, a man who was full of leprosy saw Jesus; and he fell on his face and implored Him, saying, 'Lord, if You are willing, You can make me clean.' Then He put out His hand and touched him, saying, 'I am willing; be cleansed.' Immediately the leprosy left him. And He charged him to tell no one, 'but go and show yourself to the priest,

and make an offering for your cleansing, as a testimony to them, just as Moses commanded.'" (Luke 5:12-14 NKJV)

I bring to your attention that when we come to Christ, just as this leper was full of leprosy, we are full of hurt, pain, disappointments, anger, bitterness, strife, anxiety, trauma, sexual proclivities, gender challenges, and/or addictions. I know I was. I was full of animosity, jealousy, wrath, confusion, rejection, shame, and trauma also. What were your issues when you came to Christ that you were "full of"? Luke 5:12 says that this man was "full of Leprosy." The parallel account in Matthew 8:2 describes the leper as coming to Jesus worshipping, and Mark 1:40 said that the leper came to Jesus imploring Him and kneeling down before Him. But Luke the physician gives the description of what it was like to look upon the leper, not just simply how he came to Jesus, although this matters also. My point is that when the leper came imploring and worshipping Jesus, he came full of leprosy. Leprosy was a detestable disease which had no known cure during Biblical days.[5] Due to the severity of the disease, over time it would manifest itself as numbness within the body, white, scaly, itchy skin, and eventually the loss of limbs such as feet, toes, and/or fingers. Leprous individuals quickly became an outcast from their communities as they were commanded to leave their home and family and find shelter in the wilderness or a leprous colony. Unfortunately, due to them being an outcast, the leper would have to stand far from other people who may be approaching them unaware and yell out "Unclean, unclean!"

Can you imagine not only the physical but also the mental and emotional torment these people had to endure before Christ? You would be full of sickness, watching your body change with skin ailments becoming excruciatingly visible, your limbs falling off, and you would not have help available from anyone. You would actually

---

[5] https://www.bible-history.com/backd2/leprosy.html

be banned from everyone, including your family and your community. You would be commanded to be around people who looked like you, moaned like you, and hurt just like you without any help... until Jesus. The leprous man saw Jesus. He saw salvation, the only help that was possible for him. He recognized Jesus and immediately fell on his face and begged Jesus saying, "Lord if You are willing, You can make me clean." Scripture says that Jesus touched him and assured him that "I am willing, be cleansed." With that one touch, the leprous man was cleansed and healed of the leprosy.

Now, during that time according to the Levitical Laws, men or women were not allowed to touch someone who was unclean, an outcast of the community, or diagnosed by the priest as having leprosy. If they did so, they were to receive the same fate: labelled as unclean and banished from the community. But Jesus, in His compassion and with His authority, touched the man. With that one touch He cleansed his body that had been full of leprosy.

Just as the man was full of leprosy, sometimes we, too, are full of that which has caused us to be unclean. Whatever we were full of has caused us to be separated from our families, our communities and separated from God, so that we find ourselves being an outcast, different, rejected, and neglected by those who we feel should help us. We are full of anger, we are full of bitterness, we are full of disappointment, we are full of rejection, we are full of shame, and we are full of guilt.

In my own life, I was full of addiction proclivities but one day, more than 33 years ago, Jesus touched me. It was just one touch, and I, too, was cleansed of my infirmity. Only God knows how long it had been since the leprous man in Luke 5 had actually felt or experienced the touch from another human being. That is why it was so very compassionate and loving that this is the first thing that the Lord does, even before answering or speaking to him – He touched him. That was the deepest point of his need – the feel of another's intentional touch. Jesus intentionally touched him, then He said, "Be cleansed" in answer to the leper's prayer.

My dear friend Bishop James R. Izzard, Jr., former senior pastor of Life Builders COG, would often say to us during a passionate plea after one of his sermons, "All it takes is just one touch." The Lord can touch you so intimately and so deeply where no one else can touch you, and His touch will make all the difference. I remember Bishop Izzard saying this to us and it was life changing to me: "Christ will put His finger directly on your issue. You are crying, upset, and going through the motions trying to figure out what is wrong, then the Lord comes in during that time of prayer and places his finger exactly on the issue that is tormenting you." Hallelujah! The Lord has come into my life, and I believe He has come into your life. He has placed His finger on our issues. He has touched me and you in a specific way that has brought about healing and deliverance in an area. You might have other issues or challenges to deal with, but that issue right there is gone by the authority in Jesus' name!

Beloved, dear and precious friend, what issue or issues have you been dealing with? Are they issues that have caused delayed growth or a hindrance to continue growth and development to your physical, emotional, or mental well-being? Does your life seem full of issues, so much that you may seem like an outcast to your own family and friends? Many years ago, friend, this was me. I was so very full of my issues that my issues consumed me and delayed what was supposed to be normative and developmental in my life.

I say to you that the presence and the Word of Almighty God our Lord can place His finger on that issue in your life, and it can be cleansed and healed. Allow the Lord, the Almighty God, to do this. It is yours, just for the asking. You may already be asking it in your heart; whisper those words and allow healing to come. Healing is just a whisper away.

Layer Four ~ Unhealthy Exposure

My story of unhealthy exposure in a different manner begins when I was maybe in the 4th or 5th grade, and I was friends with a girl who was around my age; I will call her Wilma. Wilma had a large family, and they always appeared to be just as unruly and un-kept as I was. Her mom was probably louder than the loudspeakers in the school's hallway and our classroom; however, I mean no disrespect at all. I believe it is very important that we get a snapshot of the type of environment Wilma had grown up in and was accustomed to. Like me, there was no father nor father figure in the home, so at the very least, we connected at that level.

Wilma and I shared the same teacher and similar physical situations that I now see, looking back over that period of time, were traps that the enemy of both of our souls played on and drew us together. I was often bullied in school due to my un-kept appearance and although Wilma was quite un-kept as well, she, her brothers, and her sisters were often the bullies that frightened others, including me. She was loud and disruptive, but again so was I. We played together both in school and at her apartment. She lived a few buildings from my family's apartment building. Instead of going home after school as I was supposed to, I would often follow Wilma to her home, and her mother and her other brothers and sisters would always be there. I often thought it better to go to her house than to go to my house because in a very strange way, her house provided somewhat of a place of protection from what I silently endured at my own home.

One day after school, we were playing in her bedroom that she shared with her sisters. I do not remember how we both ended up in the closet, but there we were. Being inside of that closet, we began to whisper and share secrets. Funny thing was, I was sharing all of my secrets; she, not so much. In those days, there were closets that connected one bedroom to another bedroom. She began to tell me stories of when one of her brothers would have girls over their house and in his room. She would get into her closet, which connected his bedroom to her bedroom, and she would watch them kiss, fondle each other, and sometimes go even further. She would tell me these stories, and then one day, she began to do to me what she had seen her brother do to his girlfriend. She would also tell me that his girlfriend would do a certain thing and that I should do that thing to her. When I would draw back, she would say to me, "You want to be liked, don't you?" I would say "Yeah, sure," thinking everybody wants to be liked, right? Well, I did. I wanted to be liked. I wanted a friend. I wanted to belong. Unfortunately, I did not know; I did not realize the price that I was being asked to pay to be liked or to be friends with Wilma, nor the price of what I was being exposed to.

The enemy was enlarging the door of unhealthy exposure in my life through my eye gates, my ear gates, and through my sensory gates. This was a similar context but also very different, as this was sexual exposure of the same gender. Another young girl like me was exposing me to the touch of another girl. The enemy had already exposed me to unhealthy touching, manipulation, and penetration as a child by a family member, and now the enemy was expanding his territory of destruction in my life. This type of episode did not happen on a daily basis with Wilma at her house, but when it would happen, I would leave and go home to my own apartment in such a state of confusion. Unfortunately, I was never confused enough that I stopped being friends with her, told my mom what was happening, nor told her mother or anyone else in authority. Honestly, I did not see anything wrong with what was being done to me or what I was being told (instructed) to do to her.

That is the lie and the root of unhealthy exposure the enemy tries to plant within us. Due to me being molested and exposed to the touching and penetration of my private areas much earlier in my childhood by a family member, I had no clue that what was being done to me was wrong, even in this way. I did not trust nor believe my feelings, even those feelings that said this does not feel right. When she would say to me, "You want to be liked, don't you?" I just thought there were things you did to be liked, and I so wanted to be liked, therefore I did those things. I did not know that I was not being liked but used, misused, having my innocence stolen, and being lied to, all under the cover of friendship and that old, unprotected umbrella of a relative's touching/handling of a child gone awry.

In thinking back to those times, I was confused about how I felt. Although I cannot remember much of it now, I often wonder why I never spoke up for myself. Was I afraid? If I was afraid, did I recognize it as fear? Was I afraid of the person(s) who were doing these ungodly acts to me, or was I afraid of the act itself? Was I simply afraid to speak up?

As I am recalling different episodes, the Holy Spirit is bringing healing both to my heart and to my mind. The Holy Spirit is allowing me to address the episodes, admitting the incidents to myself, and both forgiving and releasing myself and the parties involved, where appropriate. Even if I have to do it over and over again, this is where the healing happens: forgiving myself, accepting myself and the age of the incident, and not holding bitterness nor anger because of the loss of my childhood during those times. I have accepted the fact that God is more than willing to repay the shame of my youth and the memories that try to haunt me and locate me in places of shame, depression, and regret. The Holy Spirit washes over all of our bad memories and our bad choices, even those that we may not be able to fully recall or remember and He restores healing and health to our mind and our hearts.

Isaiah 61:7 (NKJV) says: *"Instead of your shame you shall have double honor, and instead of confusion they shall rejoice in their portion. Therefore in their land they shall possess double; everlasting joy shall be theirs."* Receive this promise for yourself and meditate upon this Scripture until it begins to peel away every layer of shame and oppression off of your life, off of your mind, and off of your heart so that you can breathe fresh air and no longer be stifled nor hindered. I hold this Scripture close to my heart and even now continue to meditate on the promise that it holds. Instead of the shame that I endured, the shame that I carried around like another garment attached to me, I thank God that the promise is that I will have double honor.

My shame may not look like your shame. My shame may sound embarrassing or uneasy to discuss or talk about, write about, or even read. It took me well over 30 years to write this book. I know what it is to carry shame, dishonor, and regret, to feel out of place for absolutely no reason at all, and to have the largest smile on my face and still go home alone and broken because of past mistakes and the shame that they caused. But God said, you are coming out of this, and I am robing you in double honor.

As you, dear friend, walk through your own places of shame and devastation, I pray God's divine healing love would wrap and cocoon you tightly. Even if you feel that you have to put the book down and come back, do so, but I beg of you to please pick it up again, come back, and receive all of the healing that Father desires to give to you. Isaiah 54:4 (NKJV) says: *"Do not fear, for you will not be ashamed; Neither be disgraced, for you will not be put to shame; For you will forget the shame of your youth, And will not remember the reproach of your widowhood anymore."* My dear friend, that's a good Word right there to hold onto.

Thankfully, we moved away from those apartments. If the walls could talk in those buildings, I am sure they would tell stories of interrupted lives and disturbed childhood dreams of many children, teens, and adults. I am sure I was not the only child that experienced these catastrophes. Because of our move to a new area, I never saw Wilma nor any other member of her family again. Unfortunately, the work that the enemy desired to do was planted in my mind, my heart, and my life: the seed of unhealthy exposure. A door was further opened that day in Wilma's bedroom closet. The door of unhealthy exposure expanded in my life and would take me down several unhealthy paths in life.

I moved away from the "Wilmas" of my life; however, I was still in the grips of my abusive family member. When we moved, unfortunately, he moved with us. We moved into a house that eventually became home to me and my family. That new home was where I would complete 6th grade and go on to middle school, high school, and even a short semester in college. That house had walls, rooms, upstairs, downstairs, and a basement. That was a new level for us as it was the first house that my mom had lived in, and it was hers; she was so proud and grateful for that house! She had every reason to be. We were "moving on up!" However, due to the opened areas of exposure, the enemy followed me mentally, emotionally, and physically into the new house and to my new schools.

I was exposed to some things, but those things brought me to where I am now. I am writing to tell others about my past experiences and how they can shed some light and perhaps bring about deliverance and peace in the lives of many who made mistakes, experienced unwelcomed exposures, and/or delayed growths they may have been through. It has been a long road to telling my story, but my mouth is open wide, and I will no longer be silent. Listen intently as I continue to peel the layers of my life away from the bandages and the masks that have kept me from speaking up and speaking out. What mask? What bandages? The masks and bandages are shame, disillusionment, low self-esteem, low self-worth, rejection, and so many other dysfunctions that were brought on by generational curses, family dysfunction, and my own disobedience, rebellion, ignorance, and defiance (hard-headedness).

I did not realize how shackled I really was. I was shackled in my emotions, my mind, and my heart, and these shackles represented imprisonment that the enemy had cast upon me. For many years, even as a Believer in Christ, I was in bondage. The shackles appeared in the spirit as chains that were on my wrists and hands, blinders on my eyes, cotton balls in my ears preventing and constraining me from hearing precisely and moving forward, all the while working to destroy me bitterly and keeping me ignorant of their true purposes, preventing my ultimate destiny.

However, God had plans for my life from the foundations of the earth. Jeremiah 29:11 has new meaning to me and for me now, as it should have for you! When you discover that God really does have a plan for your life and He desires that you would arise, hear, and see His plan, receive His plan, and begin to work His plan for your life, your life takes on new meaning and purpose. It is almost as though the chains become as wax – they melt away from your heart, your wrists, your hands, your emotions, and your mind. The cotton balls that once filled your ears and prevented you from hearing wisdom, sound advice, and heart-directed correction and discipline are now blown away by the gentle breeze of the Holy Spirit blowing fresh wind, causing you to hear the rhythms and flow of His Spirit anew. Because of the Holy Spirit gracing your life with people who sincerely love and care for you, you find people coming after you and loving on you as though their very lives depended on it. I see Jude 1:23 (NLT) in a whole new light now: *"Rescue others by snatching them from the flames of judgment. Show mercy to still others, but do so with great caution, hating the sins that contaminate their lives."*

I have experienced genuine saints of the Most-High God literally pulling me out of the flames that tried to burn up my life and destiny. These saints were genuinely concerned for my well-being and did not let me go on my own, even though I thought I knew everything. With their prayers, they often pulled me to safety and loved me to a place of healing. That is my desire in this book and its companion devotional – to meet you through Christ, right there at the place where you are, and say to you, "I have been that low before and Christ pulled me up, out, in, and through, and He can do the same for you, if you would let Him."

The unhealthy exposures that were plans derived from the enemy of your soul and sent to destroy you have been thwarted by God! They may have touched your life, but they do not have to stop you from living. The unhealthy exposures of our lives can thrust us toward the Holy Spirit and cause us to render ourselves totally submitted to Him for divine exposure. Divine exposure is when the Holy Spirit comes into your life, reveals His promises and purposes for your life, and lets you know that your story does not have to end where you thought it was over. I thought my story was over with molestation. The Holy Spirit says, "If you turn your story of molestation, your story of pain, your story of fear, even your story of doubt and unbelief over to Me, I will turn what appeared to be hell's torture into a glorious testimony! If you turn your story of unhealthy exposure, abuse, shame, rebellion and even discontent over to Me, I will turn what seemed as dirty water raining in your life, which poisoned everyone, into a well where only sweet wine will flow continuously." John 7:38 (NKJV) declares, *"He who believes in Me, as the Scripture has said, out of his heart will flow rivers of living water."*

I learned to turn my life, my heartaches, my pain, my emotional torment, and my physical discontent over to the Lord. He gladly made the wonderful exchange as only He, in His love and kindness, could. He exchanged my many sorrows and has given me unspeakable joy. He made the divine exchange in my life real. Psalm 30:11 (NKJV) says, *"You have turned my mourning into dancing; You have put off my sackcloth and clothed me with gladness."* Through His word, He has changed my thought life, my heart life, and my spirit life. He has given me a new perspective that continues to be renewed by the daily intake and reading of His word and spending time in His presence, moments of silence, and "sweet spots" as coined by Bishop Jentzen Franklin – times of enraptured glory worshipping and listening as He breathes upon me.

Change can come for you too, friend. But, how badly do you want it? How badly do you really want change? Do you want temporary change, or do you want everlasting change? In order for this type of change to occur, Christ's supernatural change that we all need to take place and experience in our lives, you have to want it.

The Lord can literally abolish every unhealthy exposure, and you can finally be healed, not forgotten but forgiven and covered by the blood of Jesus. Because of your new life in Christ, you are healed, and your life is turned around, and you are made to be so much better *in spite* of the unhealthy exposures of your past. The plans from the enemy were sent like missiles with your mind and your family as their target, but God aborted the plans. Christ is moving forward with His plan for your life – this is Jeremiah 29:11 in action, the movement over your life and destiny. God's plans are not thwarted. Look at where you are. You are on your way, and God is not finished yet. You have so much to accomplish in your life. Whatever exposures you have experienced, be they unhealthy or unexpected, God has the final say, just as he says in Romans 8:28-30 (NKJV) *"28 And we know that all things work together for good to those who love God, to those who are the called according to His purpose. 29 For whom He foreknew, He also predestined to be conformed to the image of His Son, that He might be the firstborn among many brethren. 30 Moreover whom He predestined, these He also called; whom He called, these He also justified; and whom He justified, these He also glorified."*

Why I Stayed There

Layer Five ~ Self Esteem

"Dance, Nae-Nae!" shouted one of my aunts from a smoke-filled room. Although the room felt brisk and cool, I can still remember the smell of Kool cigarettes and Budweiser beer. Every now and again, I'd get a hint of something stronger, but I did not know what that smell was; it was probably gin and orange juice or rum and coke. My mom was having a card party, and the living room of our apartment was filled with people, loud voices, and music. Card tables were in the middle of the living room floor and in almost every corner. Plates of potato salad were floating by with fried chicken and green beans, and someone yelled from across the room, "That one is mine." That was one of the ways Momma used to raise a few extra dollars, by having a card party and selling dinners. For entertainment, the kids would hear a familiar song on the record-player, and we would dance. Before long, we would be competing in dance against one another for a quarter or fifty cents; whoever was winning at the card game paid the most for us to dance.

    I remember one card party that began filled with fun but ended with me being faced with issues that I would deal with throughout the rest of my young life and into adulthood regarding my hair and my scalp. This particular card party began just like the others, however, when my cousins and I had finished dancing, we headed towards the kitchen with our pockets jingling with quarters, dimes, and nickels. We would get some food from Momma and head back to one of the bedrooms, whichever one did not have a lot of coats on the bed. After eating and getting bored as there was nothing on TV late at night, my cousin decided she was going to do something with my hair. We began to play the game of beauty shop.

My aunts would always be doing somebody's hair in their kitchen, so we knew about playing beauty shop. Ladies would come to my aunt's apartment with their hair tied up and leave with a fresh perm, finger waves, or a roller set. Momma was never big on hair, though, neither in perming nor platting. I often had one plat on the top of my head, falling over the side of my head towards one of my ears, and one plat held by a rubber-band in the back of my head. I finally outgrew the two plats sticking straight up from my head, which made me look like I had antennas. I was teased by my brothers and called a praying mantis, but I finally outgrew that stage.

I had a whole lot of knotted, nappy hair in my "kitchen area" (in the back of my head, at the base of my neck) and Momma would just leave it alone because I was very tender-headed as a child. Momma did not send me to my aunts to get my hair done because she knew how tender-headed I was. Momma would say, "I don't see the need in transporting you across town to have your hair done for you to sit in the chair and scream and holler the entire time," so that never happened.

I guess my cousin got tired of looking at my BBs (that's what we used to call girls' hair that was nappy and unkept in the kitchen area). So, she said, "Let's play beauty shop," and she made me her client. Honestly, I don't know where she got that paint can nor the paint brush, but before long she had taken my plats loose and was "perming" my hair with the white paint. She covered my entire head with white paint. I guess to her, it really did look and smell like a perm. It felt yucky. With all the paint dripping from my hair onto my clothes and down my back, when I would try to wipe it off, I would get paint everywhere I wiped. My hair was too thick, and the comb was not going through so she kept asking me, "Is it burning yet?" I said no because it was not burning. So, we kept playing and having conversations about the neighbors, much like my aunts when they had clients. They would talk about the people in the neighborhood and so we did the same thing. "Girl, did you see so and so? Honey, did you hear about such and such?"

We kept it going until the comb she was using would not comb through my hair. She said, "Well, it's time to wash you out." I thought, *Wash me out? I ain't gonna let her wash my hair.* She took me to the bathroom, and she put my head under the running water in the sink. I started screaming and she, still playing the game, said, "Girl, I'm just about finished washing you out… wait… wait! Don't cry." I was screaming as loud as I could.

Momma came to the bathroom door and started yelling and cursing. "What da? What are y'all doing?" Momma's yelling turned into fussing at both of us. I guess the beauty shop game was over, although the card party was still in full swing. I thought Momma would be able to get me out of there and away from my cousin, but instead, the water was warmed up more at her attempts to rinse the paint from my hair. I cannot tell you how long this took. Things continued to get worse instead of better, and white paint was everywhere, not only on me but everywhere in the bathroom. Momma moved me from the sink to the bathtub. She started pouring so much water on my hair that I found myself sitting in a tub of hot water and white paint.

Everybody had an idea as to how to get that paint out of my hair, according to Momma telling the story months after it all happened and even as I got older. It was the funny story at family gatherings. "Girl, we tried everything, and nothing worked. Dagonnit nappy hair!"

Well, nothing did work, and momma ended up cutting off all my hair. I was bald for months until fuzz began to grow back, and then for good measure, I turned around and caught ringworms. I think the enemy had it out for my hair, too. Finally, after the ringworms, my hair began to grow back; however, it was never like it was before the white paint and the ringworms. My hair grew back in patches. Out of desperation and me getting older and complaining that I wanted to look pretty like the other girls at school, Momma resorted to a Vigorol

Relaxer. They were thought to be not as strong as a perm. However, because I did not take care of myself or my hair, my hair began to break off.

Then we resorted to perms, which were a bad idea. I remember coming from the salon that one of my mom's friends had near my mom's office. It was times like these that I loved going to work and missing school so that I could be with my mom. Momma would sometimes let me sit at the receptionist desk, and occasionally the receptionist would let me answer the phone. This particular time, I was there to visit the hair salon. While there, the stylist put a perm in my hair. After she had finished my hair, she turned the chair that I was sitting in to face the mirror and I could have sworn that there was somebody else sitting in the chair. I had no idea I had so much hair! Although my hair was still short, the perm straightened it out quite a bit. When I got home, I could not wait to show my friends. I was so excited about them seeing me and how cute I was, or how cute I thought I was.

When I knocked on the door to my friend's house, she opened the door and started screaming. "LisaPate!" She said my name as though it was one syllable, the first and last name running together. "LisaPate! Girl, what did you do to your hair? Girl, is that a wig you wearing? Girl, your hair looks so good!" Again, she asked me, "Is that a wig? It looks like it's a wig."

I answered, "No, it is not a wig. My mom took me to the salon."

My friend called out to her mom, and her sisters came running for good measure. "Hey Ma, come see LisaPate's hair. She got on a wig and she trying to say it's her hair. Come see; hurry up!" Her mother and her sisters came.

I heard her mother say, "If it is a wig, I'll know it; I'll be able to tell." She stood in front of me and began to compliment me. "Wow! Look at you, LisaPate. Your hair looks so nice. You say you got a perm, huh? Let me take a look." Right then and there, she began poking her fingers through the curls of my scalp so as to feel if it was a wig or not. Tears welled up in my eyes and a knot filled my throat. I kept breathing and swallowing. I was determined that I was not going to let them see me cry. I was hurt, to say the least. Was it not okay to look good and to look nice, or at least to feel like you looked nice? Was it not okay to look nice in my own hair, permed and all, or did I have to have on a wig so that they could feel good about themselves or better than me? I continued to breathe and swallow as I had learned through other traumas. When her mom discovered that it was my hair, she stopped poking her fingers through my curls and said, "Oh yeah, it does look really nice. It is not a wig, but you make sure you take care of it." After that, my friend and I went outside to play. We played and never mentioned or talked about all that had just happened.

Looking back on those times, the perm probably would have worked for my hair if I would have had the proper care. But I did not know much of anything about taking care of myself, let alone taking care of my hair, even as I entered my tween years.

This was not the end of my hair problems. In spite of the things that were happening in my life, it was among the mounting struggles that took place dealing with self-esteem. By the time I was well into my thirties, I discovered that I had a beautiful smile; however, while growing up as a young girl and into my tween years, I had bucked teeth. One day on the way home from school, I was chased by dogs, fell, and chipped my two front teeth. They were chipped into a perfect upside down V shape. So, here I was not only with the challenges I was facing with my hair or the lack thereof, but my bucked front teeth were now chipped.

Things were not going well for me that year. With these very important features being stripped away from me, so to speak, I did not feel pretty or cute. In fact, this is where most of my rejection began devolving into self-rejection. I dealt with low or no self-esteem as a young girl in school, and I would definitely have encounters regarding my self-esteem later in life. I was also not happy with the body I was walking around in. I was narrow, with long legs and no hip bones that I could feel, although I'm sure they were there. I wanted to be cute like the other girls, but I did not know how to make that happen for me. As a young girl faced with these and other challenges, I was once again found to have a poor attitude. I did not know to look on the bright side of things because for me, there was no bright side.

A Roof Doesn't Equal Love

These were my formative years, which for me seemed to be very bitter. Yet, it is a part of my testimony, though I did not know that at that time. These were the developing stages of my story. I did not know how to tell my story or even who to share my story with. In fact, in writing this book, I am finally able to share my story in such an open and transparent way, with the heartfelt prayer that it will reach those who I may never see or those who may never see me. If you feel that as you grew up, those who should have seen you, loved you, taken care of you, and made you feel secure did not see you or were too busy with life that they did not take care of you, I get that and I do not disrespect that. They provided a roof over your head, and for them, that was love.

However, there is more to love than the shelter of a home or an apartment. The breadth, height, and width of their love for their child nourishes, protects, solidifies, and creates within the child a sense of person so great within themselves that loving themselves, their family, and their neighbors is sheer joy because they themselves are affirmed. They have grown up in and have been clothed with the benefits of life, surrounded in and by love. Oh, to have experienced this type of surrounding! It is possible. I have seen it and I have watched it from afar. I am not talking about the kind of love whereby the parents throw money at the child; I am talking about the kind of love from the parent to the child that says you may have done something tragic, but I am walking with you through it. That is the kind of love I am talking about. This is the kind of love I believe in, and it is also the kind of love that needs to be demonstrated. This is the kind of love that says, from the parent to the child, I am in this with you, through thick and thin.

It feels like it has taken a lifetime to come to grips with my true feelings, my emotions, and coming to grips with all of the trauma. Through continuing to grow in my Christian walk and learning the awareness of who God is calling me to be as a Christian woman, mother, grandmother, sister, and friend, I am seeing through the fog of the anger, hurt, shame, guilt, disappointment, rejection, and molestation. I am not seeing why it all happened but dealing with the fact that it did all happen, and it is still working together for the good plan that the Lord has for me. From a place of joy, grace, and peace, I continue to recognize and believe that that is not who I was. Because it happened to me, it did not make me out to be all of those tag lines and those names which the enemy tried for years to deceive me into believing were my identity. I no longer believe the lie. Those were bald-faced lies that the enemy of my soul tried to convince me of for years. He had solid evidence, but just because I did it, it did not make me what I did. Just because it happened to me, it does not make me accept and lay hold to that and adopt it as part of my identity, nor behold it as who I am. I am awake now and am no longer sleeping through my life. I am listening to what the Word of God says about me, and I am actively walking in that, no longer being dictated to by my feelings, people, the whims of the culture, or the world. The thing about the enemy, people, the culture, and life is that if you do not know who you are, they are happy to dictate to you who you are and/or who you should be to them.

Throughout my years of growing and developing, especially as a Christian, I have spent a lot of hours in the chair of highly informed and well-educated psychologists, counselors, mentors, and coaches. From all of these areas, I have been advised and perhaps encouraged to have conversations, so to speak, with my younger self to bring about a measure of healing in my life, now that I am an adult. Although I laugh about it now and my current psychologist and counselor both laugh with me, I would often say to them, "My younger self never answers back, nor does she talk much." Through many counseling sessions, I have learned not to "have conversations" with my younger self but to speak to her in order to decree and declare to her and over her, realizing that I am professing and talking to my older self all the while. I am continuing to work through issues of the child within and may do so for the rest of my life, and that is okay; I accept that and I am willing and investing in the time to do so. I cannot begin to tell you how much this has helped me and continues to propel me forward, especially as I continue to move forward in life and especially as I now have the privilege and wonderful opportunity to mentor and coach other young women.

Through making these declarations that I will share with you, I am continuing to walk in greater depths of these truths according to the Word of God. Because I believe the Word of God, I move my feelings and my emotions out of the way; I pull them down and no longer allow them to take control and tell me how I am going to feel about a situation or a person. Your emotions and your limited knowledge about a circumstance and/or situation will keep you hindered, hemmed up, and "prohibited" from stepping out of the box of who you were as a child, young tween, teenager, or young adult. I say to you, STOP listening to how you <u>used</u> to feel. Allow yourself to breathe and believe who you are in God! In order for you to believe who God says you are in His Word, you have to learn His Word and what it says about you. I took this challenge several years ago and have grown all the more because of it.

I have learned to see emotional traumas as emotional traps. Emotional traps come and place holds on our mind, hands, feet, and destiny. This ought not to be; you can let go of the hold! Sometimes, you are holding your own self back. No longer allow your present self to look to, feel, think, or even imagine things from the perspective of what you have been through. I am not telling you to deny what happened or the feelings you felt before, either during or years after it happened. Do not allow what happened, how you felt about what happened, or how you felt during and/or years after it happened to stop you from moving forward in life.

One of the things I did, that I am so very glad I did, was reaching out to both a psychologist and counselor who began to lead and direct me into a healthy relationship with myself and others so that I could live my life to its fullest. Now, friend, grab a hold of your past emotional trauma, walk through it with a counselor and/or psychologist who will help you to embrace it, and use every last bit of all that happened to you to make you better. This can work for you, too; I know it can.

Friend, I'll be honest with you; after all these years, I am discovering with the help and guidance of the Holy Spirit that those traumas that were introduced into my life by the enemy of my soul were desperately trying to deceive me into aborting the wonderful and glorious call and plans the Lord has upon and for my life. The Lord has made me so very gifted in many areas, and I work very hard to hone my gifts and crafts so that I am bringing to the Lord my best and not just being busy – falling into another one of the enemy's traps of being busy but not effective nor productive. But I had to learn the niches which the Lord has crafted me with. I had to spend time with Him and learning, falling, and being willing to get back up and begin again. The lessons were not easy; they never will be, and thank the Lord that they are not. Ask yourself: do you genuinely appreciate things that are easy and/or less challenging? Do things that are easy serve you or propel you forward? I have grown to appreciate the lessons I have learned that were challenging and not so easy. They are serving me well. Learn to allow them to do so for you. One of the lessons that I have learned the hard way and that proved to be quite challenging for me was being myself.

You Are YOU

We have turned into a culture that tweaks our selfie photos and plasters them on many different social media platforms; however, we will not dare to put up a selfie/post unless it has been "retouched" to make it look better than our natural selves. I have learned over the last 10 years to love my skin tone, my laugh (which is robust), the way I walk, my ease with people who do not look or sound like me, and after 10 years, my hair and I have come to terms; I like her and she loves me. I have accepted my broad shoulders, my wide back, my lack of hips, my wide nose, and my teeth, especially after I had the v-shape repaired. My teeth are still a little "buck," but it makes my smile even more beautiful.

Here is why I went into such great detail to tell you the things that I am accepting and enjoying about me. I would be willing to surmise that there are women and men reading this book who have not come to grips with your skin complexion, the moles that have sprang up from nowhere on your face and neck, etc. Perhaps you have always had a thing that the lobes of your ears were too long, or that your lips were too large or too narrow or maybe even to dark for your skin tone. You may have even tried to tone down who you really are. Maybe you, too, have a robust laugh; perhaps you are a bit on the loud side and your friends have always said to you, "We hear you before we see you." This has provoked a calculated effort on your part to change this about you, and you have begun adapting and adjusting who you really are into who you believe people want to see: this calm, and cool person is a totally different version of who you are sincerely.

Friend, you have been squeezing who you are into the mold that the culture, your present friends, your job, and/or your social media friends have dictated that you should be. Believe me, you cannot change who you really are to be friends or to get along with and be accepted by someone who really does not know or like who you are at your core. Who you really are is God's gift to everyone around you. Who you really are and who you are growing to be in the Lord is God's gift to you and everyone around you. I am talking to the person who has accepted the fact that God says to you through His word. Ephesians 2:10 (NLT) says, *"For we are God's masterpiece. He has created us anew in Christ Jesus, so we can do the good things He planned for us long ago."*

Now, if you have not accepted the Lord nor His word for your life, my prayer is that by the end of this book, you will. Until then, let me say this to you. It matters that you accept the fullness of who you are. If you try to "bend" your gifts or fit who you are at your core into the box of comfort for people's sake, the box of normality for people's sake, or the box of comparison for people's sake, it limits how God can express Himself through you. It may be challenging for you to be your authentic self but that is the best self that you can be. This is what I have come to know about the God that we serve; the Lord desires you to be your **full** self, your authentic and bold self, in order for Him to express Himself thoroughly and freely without constraints in your life. I say this to you in such a loving way, yet boldly declaring in your hearing: "You're not everybody else! You're not somebody else! ***You are YOU*!**"

Think about all that you have gone through, come through, endured through, and suffered through to be who you are and to get to this point in your life. To deny that would be absolutely criminal and says to God that He does not know what He is doing. Isaiah 45:9 (NLT) says, *"What sorrow awaits those who argue with their Creator. Does a clay pot argue with its maker? Does the clay dispute with the one who shapes it, saying, 'Stop, you're doing it wrong!' Does the pot exclaim, 'How clumsy can you be?'"* Romans 9:20 (NKJV) says, *"No, don't say that. Who are you, a mere human being, to argue with God? Should the thing that was created say to the one who created it, 'Why have you made me like this?'"* Beloved, we do not argue with our Creator. We accept the fine and beautiful person that He has made us to be; after all, He did form us in our mother's womb.

However, your beauty may not be outward. Your handsomeness may not be outward. Does that mean that you are not worthy to be who God made you to be? Certainly not. The world that we live in, especially this current culture, depends so much on the outward features of a person. The culture measures and compares these outward features with who you are as a person against other people. It attempts to measure and/or make you find value in yourself or another person simply by what is seen. This should not be. This is why so many people (models, cover girls, movie actors, etc.) are comparing their looks or their monetary value with others and committing suicide when they feel as though they do not measure up. Unfortunately, most are becoming alcoholics and drug addicts because they cannot stand the pressures of that comparison nor the stringent and overwhelmingly challenging lifestyle that they have had to "fit in" in order to run with and be in the same league or friendship with this type of folks.

Beloved, it is wrong and unacceptable and we do ourselves a disservice when we settle to compare ourselves, our looks, our weight, our features, our hair, our hairline, our gifts, our talents, our service, our achievements, and certainly our anointing and ministries to other people, whether brothers and sisters in this culture or in the Kingdom of God. Each person has the unique capability to allow the light of God's love and personality to shine through their heart. Every person possesses a unique perspective (their lens) that God uses to touch, serve, and minister to people that we come into contact with on a moment-by-moment basis. He uses our individuality, our experiences, our history, and the lessons we have learned from our history, especially the history that has been redeemed by the blood of Jesus.

God desires to use every bit of our story to reach the next person and the next generation. But if we are condemning our story and comparing our story, not believing that God even desires to use our story because it does not sound, look like, or measure up to someone else's story, how can we reach anyone? How can we be a conduit through which Christ can show, give, and express His love here on earth? Remember, we are no longer fitting ourselves into the box or mold of this culture, allowing the culture to mold and shape us into what it wants or needs us to be for them. No! We are formed into the image God has already made for us; we are walking in His love and His light, and we are experiencing and reflecting His Life in the world, even our very culture. Romans 12:2 (NKJV) says: *"And do not be conformed to this world, but be transformed by the renewing of your mind, that you may prove what is that good and acceptable and perfect will of God."* <u>The same verse from the New Living translation</u> says: *"Don't copy the behavior and customs of this world, but let God transform you into a new person by changing the way you think. Then you will learn to know God's will for you, which is good and pleasing and perfect."*

Low Self-Esteem Is Not Inherited

Now that we have conquered the enemy of comparison, the next step is to note that you were not born with low self-esteem. Low self-esteem and low self-worth are the deception of the enemy that we grow into, believing the lie of the enemy that we are not "enough." We grow into believing that we are not tall enough, we are not short enough, we are not pretty enough, we are not thin enough, we are not fat (or phat) enough, our hair is not straight enough, or our hair is not long enough. Some have even believed the centuries-old lie about "good hair" and therefore have adopted the concept that they do not have "good hair."

We grow into the lie that we are not enough. We grow into the deception that often comes from the words of family members who may not have liked us or who may have been jealous of us. Or perhaps so-called friends may have said, "Your forehead is too big or long for your face." These kinds of sayings hurt us at our core. If we did not have a foundational base of love to fight such sayings off, these formed within us low self-esteem or low self-worth, which was continuously fed by the enemy of our souls. However, we must stop comparing ourselves to others. We must stop listening to the lies of those who are being used by the enemy to plant deceptive thoughts in our ears that say to us that we are not enough. We must stop believing and receiving the old narrative about ourselves, and we must allow it to be redeemed by Christ. Christ died for such a purchase as the old narrative that we constantly reflect on and try to bring into our current situations. Once and for all, stop believing the lie and stop rehearsing it. Stop allowing old memory scenes to play over and over again in your heart and in your head.

I have experienced growing up without a father or a father figure in the home, molestation at a young age, delayed growth, unhealthy exposures to sexuality issues, drug abuse, single parenting, remaining unmarried for more than 26 years while in the church, being groomed and mentored into leadership. My experiences have given me my unique perspective. My lenses are varied, wide, and far-reaching; God can use these to reach people whom others may never see and or feel compelled to witness to or touch. Although God did not choose the situations and circumstances that I have been through, He does choose to use them, each and every one of them, for His glory to reach people for His Kingdom.

Scriptures of Declarations & Decrees

1 Samuel 16:7 (NKJV) *"But the LORD said to Samuel, 'Do not look at his appearance or at his physical stature, because I have refused him. For the LORD does not see as man sees; for man looks at the outward appearance, but the LORD looks at the heart.'"*

Psalm 139:14 (NKJV) *"I will praise You, for I am fearfully and wonderfully made; Marvelous are Your works, And that my soul knows very well."*

1 John 3:1 (NLT) *"See how very much our Father loves us, for He calls us His children, and that is what we are! But the people who belong to this world don't recognize that we are God's children because they don't know Him."*

Jeremiah 1:6-8 (NKJV) *⁶ "Then said I: 'Ah, Lord God! Behold, I cannot speak, for I am a youth.' ⁷ But the LORD said to me: 'Do not say, I am a youth,' For you shall go to all to whom I send you, And whatever I command you, you shall speak. ⁹ Do not be afraid of their faces, For I am with you to deliver you, says the LORD."*

Exodus 4:10-12 (NKJV) *¹⁰ "Then Moses said to the LORD, 'O my Lord, I am not eloquent, neither before nor since You have spoken to Your servant; but I am slow of speech and slow of tongue.' ¹¹ So the LORD said to him, 'Who has made man's mouth? Or who makes the mute, the death, the seeing, or the blind? Have not I the LORD? ¹² Now therefore, go, and I will be with your mouth and teach you what you shall say.'"*

1 Peter 2:9 (NKJV) *"But you are a chosen generation, a royal priesthood, a holy nation, His own special people, that you may proclaim the praises of Him who called you out of darkness into His marvelous light."*

Zephaniah 3:17 (NKJV) *"The Lord your God in your midst, The Mighty One, will save; He will rejoice over you with gladness, He will quiet you with His love, He will rejoice over you with singing."*

Layer Six ~ Shame, Rejection, and Guilt

Shame

Shame will grab you by your neck and hold you up so high that your feet are off the ground, and you are no longer able to walk nor take a step. While this choke hold is cutting off your life's air, your vision is obscured. You do not see things as you should. Everything you are capturing, seeing, and receiving is through the grips of shame. But God…

> *⁴ But God is so rich in mercy, and he loved us so much,*
> *⁵ that even though we were dead because of our sins, he gave us life when he raised Christ from the dead. (It is only by God's grace that you have been saved!)*
> *⁶ For he raised us from the dead along with Christ and seated us with him in the heavenly realms because we are united with Christ Jesus.*
> *⁷ So God can point to us in all future ages **as examples** of the incredible wealth of his grace and kindness toward us, as shown in all he has done for us who are united with Christ Jesus.*
> *⁸ **God saved you by his grace when you believed. And you can't take credit for this; it is a gift from God.***
>   Ephesians 2:4-8 (NLT, emphasis mine)

The spirit of shame had such a stronghold in and on my life that I began to believe it would never release its grip. Its grip seemed to be endless, almost like an octopus' tentacles. It was not just one grip; it was several grips, deep within my soul. The root or the foundational grip of shame was planted deep within my life several weeks after I met a young man at a night club. This young man was intelligent, worked a good job, and seemed to be "together" in his mind. But who really knows the mind and the heart of a man? Only the Lord God. There was nothing about this young man's stature, place in life, demeanor, or the way that he carried himself that spoke of him being a drug dealer, but he was. To me, looking back on how things were then, he probably could have been considered among the worst of drug dealers – an unsuspected one. Yet, in all of my brokenness, I was attracted to him. As we dated and drew close to one another, it was not an immediate capturing of my heart; it was very, very subtle. It started with encouraging trust and dependency. The trust was needed so that I would trust whatever he said or did; however, the dependency followed suit almost immediately.

I was a young single mother at this point in my life. My first-born son, my only child at that time was my life, was my love and the reason that I lived and smiled. I did not realize that feeling could be snatched away in a heartbeat, but life was about to visit me in a very unreal way. I was horribly unprepared.

My beautiful son was born by C-section. His dad saw him before I did. When the nurse handed him to us both, our eyes released what was in our hearts. We cried upon our first glimpse of him. He was (and still is) the epitome of beauty to us both. I was still living at home with my mom, and when I brought our new bundle of joy home, our home became alive with joy. During this season, my mom was so loving and caring to my son, her new grandson. To see her with him felt like a new connection was seamlessly woven between me and her. Tangible love was intensified and experienced by everyone who came to our house. I grew from carrying him with such great joy and anticipation in my womb to nursing him and loving every moment of it. Seeing him and feeling our eyes melt into one another as we bonded, especially as he nursed at my breast, was the purest form of love and something that I had never experienced; it was simply beautiful. My son was all I needed. He was all I wanted. Over the course of time, his dad and I drifted apart and finally parted ways. I moved away from my mom's home and moved into my own apartment.

It was in this same apartment where early in my son's life joys were shared, dinners were eaten, and night lamps were turned off after a kiss on the cheek and a whisper of, "I love you this much," with arms stretched open wide, "and I love you so much more," as I would often say to him. Unfortunately, I attempted to fill what was missing in my life on my own terms, as we often do. We look for something outsides of ourselves, when actually our spirit is aching for a love relationship with Christ that can only be filled by Him. It is so unfortunate that humankind always tries to fill our empty voids with the presence of another man or woman, even if that other human being is the poorest example of a man or woman. I am not blaming anyone; I take full responsibility. But if I am fully truthful, I also blame the enemy of my soul, Satan himself. He had a stronghold in my life with all the other disadvantages I had experienced, and unfortunately, I was never fully healed nor delivered. Unfortunately, I went from one thing to the next thing and this person, this drug dealer, was the next thing.

During a night of celebrating at a birthday party we attended, cocaine was introduced to my life. I had never used cocaine before, let alone smoked crack cocaine, so this introduction to this new level of living fascinated me. This was not the beginning of the lies that the great deceiver would tell me, nor the ones I would tell myself, nor the lies I would believe in the days, weeks, and months that followed. Yet, because I began to trust and depend on my new boyfriend the drug dealer, the independent young lady I had been disappeared.

Perhaps my brokenness contributed to my quick addiction. It took literally days for a drastic change to occur in who I had become. I did not recognize myself. I would not eat for days on end. I managed to feed my son only by the small measure of the person of who I was, which was trying desperately to stay in control. Over time, the drugs won out, and I became totally absorbed in the addiction. My son, who was just a toddler, was being taken care of by his grandmother, his father's mom, during the week which allowed me to work (while I was working), and he would come home on the weekends.

One particular time, I was smoking cocaine continually during the week so much that when my son came home that weekend, he was in his bedroom and I was in my bedroom, and I could not shake myself away from what was utterly destroying me, the crack cocaine. Within moments, he had opened the bedroom door and saw what I was doing for the first time. He looked at me; his eyes pierced right through me. But I could not stop. I could not stop. Tears began flooding my eyes. They were rolling down my face as I was looking at him, looking at me, watching me kill myself and kill us, taking drag after drag from the crack cocaine pipe. But I could not stop.

I finally reached for the phone on my nightstand, and I knew that I did not want him to hear me, so I ran to the kitchen and reached for the phone on the wall. I called his dad and told him to come and get him. "Come and get my son, I do not want him to see me like this," was all I could say. His dad was there within moments, or at least it felt like it. He took my son to safety, away from me. I had allowed my addiction to separate me from my love, my son, my baby.

That was the beginning of my adult horror. With my son away from me, it seemed that all hell was released on me. I had no rules. Surrounded by hurt, the pain of giving up my son, and my own dysfunctions magnified, accompanied by a person who used me to work for his pleasure and his purposes selfishly, I sunk to a place from which I did not think I could crawl out of or come back from. It was not long after my son was taken to safety that I lost my apartment. When sleep would visit me, I would sleep at people's houses who I barely knew. That soon ended because my appearance dictated the kind of life I had chosen.

My family knew that my son was safe, and they simply prayed for me. My mother had not been a believer earlier in my life, however, Christ won her heart, and she knew that the family was facing something that only God could help us through. My mom prayed for me, loved me, and would look at me with eyes that seemed to say, "I know my baby is in there somewhere and I am praying for her." My sister, who was a believer for her whole life, kept me covered in the blood of Jesus, which is why the enemy's time in this particular area of my life was short lived. Even my son prayed. He was just a child, just a toddler, but his heart missed and longed for the mom that he had come to know and love.

Days turned into weeks that my son was away from me, which were days and weeks that I was on the streets. I no longer looked like a pleasing object that could be used for the drug dealer's pleasure, so he eventually moved on. I became a liability to him and his product and was no longer able to provide a service to him or his crew, so that ended abruptly and quite swiftly. It needed to end because God had other plans. I was on my own, going from place to place, house to house, and person to person. I had an addiction, and the addiction ran my entire life. I no longer tried to go home. I was too ashamed of how I looked, how I smelled, and the activity that I was performing due to the drugs. I was too ashamed to go home.

I have often heard that you can always go home, but I simply was too ashamed to even hope to go home. I had become a prostitute just to supply myself with the drugs that I thought I needed to survive. Although I never went to jail or prison, I was in the company of many who did. In that hole of a space, I came across people the likes of which I would have never suspected to be involved in such a hideous lifestyle. Yet, past all the makeup, all the foundation, and all the beautiful clothes, they were just as I was, a prostitute. Some were men, others were women. Some were tricked into selling things that they owned for drugs, only to end up just like me, selling themselves.

I was hurting deeply at my core because I was so very alone. I had a son but could not see him, not because his dad or his family would not let me but because I was too ashamed for him to see me. I had fooled myself a couple of times. I would get to a hotel with a bathroom near the reception area and I would clean myself up and appear decent enough to see my baby, but by the time I had walked halfway to their house where I knew he was staying, I would talk myself out of seeing him. The closer I got, my voice and the enemy's voice inside of me became louder and louder until the only thing that would silence the voice of shame in my ears was more drugs.

Yet, I wanted to see my baby, my son. I would lay down on cardboard boxes in abandoned buildings wishing I could see him. His face was in every day. I longed to be with him. I desired to see him, but shame held me back. Shame took on a voice in my ears and would say to me, "You hurt him once; leave him alone. He is better off without you. He is being taken care of. You will get yourself together tomorrow and you can see him then." But that "tomorrow" never came until I was in my mid-thirties, after several years of using cocaine. By that time my son was a youth, under the age of 10 or so. I had convinced myself that he was better off without me; again, shame was doing most of the convincing. I convinced myself that I had no right to come into his life and demand that he leave the family he was with and come back home with me. I made myself believe that he was better off without me; after all, he was being taken care of. Due to shame, I made myself believe a lie that I sincerely regret to this day.

Due to the prayers of my son, my mom, and my sister I was delivered from crack cocaine after more than 6 years. My deliverance came at a heavy price, though. Satan, the enemy of our souls, will never allow anyone to be robbed from his demonic kingdom without repercussions and retaliation taking place. Salvation is free, however, it is not cheap. Christ paid for my salvation, and He also paid for yours on the cross of Calvary. This was not a cheap purchase.

The Price Paid for Sin

Humankind's salvation was purchased with the precious blood of Jesus. The Roman soldiers could have placed nails in His hands and feet and placed Him on a cross to waste away and die. But instead, He had to endure torture because He was paying for the sins of mankind, taking those sins upon His body, purchasing healing of every known and unknown disease, and providing deliverance from dangers including those seen and those in the unseen world of principalities, powers, rulers, and demonic princes in high places. In fact, before Jesus was led to the crucifixion site, Pilate ordered that Jesus be scourged (see Matthew 27:26). This scourging or flogging as it was also called was a beating by Roman soldiers with a whip known as the cat-o-nine tails. This flogging instrument was a whip which was used to invoke extreme and severe punishment upon its victim. The whip was made up of 9 stems of leather flail which was covered with stones, lead balls, animal bones and metal which tore into Christ's flesh. He received 39 stripes because it was believed that a man receiving 40 would not survive. These are the stripes that He received for you and me. Matthew 27:27-31 says, *[27] Then the soldiers of the governor took Jesus into the Praetorium and gathered the whole garrison around Him. [28] And they stripped Him and put a scarlet robe on Him. [29] When they had twisted a crown of thorns, they put it on His head, and a reed in His right hand. And they bowed the knee before Him and mocked Him, saying, "Hail, King of the Jews!" [30] Then they spat on Him, and took the reed and struck Him on the head. [31] And when they had mocked Him, they took the robe off Him, put His own clothes on Him, and led Him away to be crucified.* Realizing both the scourging/flogging Christ endured for humanity's salvation and reading this passage of his beating, after the scourging/flogging, now fully aware of the suffering received by our Lord and Savior, realizing that He took this punishment, this torture, just for you and for me I now read Isaiah 53:5 more passionately as it takes on new meaning for me and I pray for you. *"But He was wounded for our transgressions, He was bruised for our iniquities; The chastisement for our peace was upon Him, And by His stripes we are healed."*

If this were not enough, Jesus still had to carry His cross through the Via Dolorosa[6], also known as the *"Sorrowful Way"* or *"Way of Suffering."* This is the road the Roman soldiers used to take Jesus to his crucifixion. Under the pressure of both the scourging/flogging, the beating and now the weight of the wooden cross itself, Christ received help by Simon, a man from Cyrene. The soldiers grabbed him from the crowd of onlookers and made him take the cross and carry it the rest of the way to Golgotha. It was at this place that they crucified our Lord of Glory.

As quoted from Steve Shirley, owner and author of www.jesusalive.cc, in his article *Can You Describe Jesus' Physical Sufferings on His Last Day*? "By the time Jesus reached the crucifixion site, He was probably in what a hospital would call 'critical condition.' At this point, His hands were nailed to the crossbeam. Another point that most scholars and historians agree upon is that 'hands' really mean 'wrists.' The hands could not have been nailed to the cross because they could not support the weight of a man's body hanging on the cross. The nail would rip right out of the hand. The wrists, however, could hold a man's weight when done properly. History seems to bear out that this was what the Romans did. The Romans had perfected this technique, driving a 5-7" nail (more like a spike) between the radius and ulna bones in the wrist and directly into the median nerve. This gave maximum strength and caused maximum pain, as well as minimal blood loss. (One source said it would be like being struck with a cattle prod that never stopped shocking[7].)"

Matthew 27:35-37 says: *"Then they crucified Him, and divided His garments, casting lots, that it might be fulfilled which was*

---

[6] https://en.wikipedia.org/wiki/Via_Dolorosa

[7] Steve Shirley, "Can You Describe Jesus' Physical Suffereings on His Last Day?" https://jesusalive.cc/jesus-sufferings-final-day/, accessed May 26, 2021.

spoken by the prophet: 'they divided My garments among them, And for My clothing they cast lots.' Sitting down, they kept watch over Him there. And they put up over His head the accusation written against Him: THIS IS JESUS THE KING OF THE JEWS." Our King, held high and arms stretched wide to receive a world that rejected Him in life, death and yes, even His resurrection. As Christ told the disciples in the Garden of Gethsemane, Matthew 27:53 (NKJV), *"Or do you think that I cannot now pray to My Father, and He will provide Me with more than twelve legions of angels."* He could have done so on the cross; however, He fulfilled His Father's will for Himself and Humanity, He endured the cross, with all of its shame and finished the work that was set before Him. Hebrews 12:2 says: *"Looking unto Jesus, the author and finisher of our faith, who for the joy that was set before Him endured the cross, despising the shame, and has sat down at the right hand of the throne of God."*

I especially felt impressed of the Lord to provide written detail regarding the crucifixion death of my Lord and Savior; especially in this chapter because so many have experienced what I dealt with. For others, drug addiction may have caused prison or jail time and even cost someone's life. My story is important, but the detailed information about the price Christ paid for our sins is so much more important! It is life changing, if accepted and received. Salvation is free, but it is not cheap.

The Road to Healing & Home

Thank God for His Son, Jesus Christ, giving His life as payment for our sins and the sins of humanity. I gave Christ's story of crucifixion in detail because as my family was praying for deliverance for me, exactly one week before Easter of that year, I was on a street corner near my mom's home hitting a crack pipe. It was broad daylight, and I was desperate, brazen, and probably driven to a point of craziness due to my addiction with crack cocaine. This was a very critical juncture for me. I had contracted a venereal disease, and although I had the money for treatment a few times, I would always end up smoking it up.

This time, though, God had had enough. I remember being sick, running a fever and still on the street smoking crack. Due to not receiving treatment for the sexually transmitted disease, it began to spread to my fallopian tubes and caused pelvic inflammatory disease. I continued to be sick on the streets, and I began to pass out. Each time I would wake up from a fainting spell, I would find myself still on the streets, with the crack pipe in my hand. This continued for a day or two. Finally, someone called an ambulance, and I was taken to a hospital. While in the emergency room, I was not able to smoke the crack that had numbed the pain my body was feeling which the fever was dictating. The pain was excruciating; however, my pain was NOTHING like the pain Christ felt during his beating with the cat-o-nine tails nor while on the cross in order to bring deliverance to me and all of humanity.

The pain I was feeling was so bad that I knelt on the floor of the emergency room, crawling to people, begging for help. I passed out, and the nurses and doctors would simply place me back on a gurney until I could be seen and properly diagnosed and admitted. Unfortunately, my bodily fluids began to do their own thing as the pain continued and I blacked out periodically. As I began to crawl on the floor and writhe with pain, I remember a janitor, a Caucasian guy with blond hair, would look at me while mopping up my bodily fluids, all the while talking to me and reassuring me that everything was going to be alright. This was the beginning of my process – everything was going to be alright.

I was finally given a room where there was no one around who could answer the call of the monkey on my back about drugs. Drugs had swiftly come into my life, destroying everything like a burning forest fire. Everything I had was burned up. Every friendship, every relationship, including the relationship with my son, was burned up in the fire of my life.

But God had had enough! The room that I was assigned to that night would give way to the transformation that God had planned by week's end. I had my first night in a clean environment, and in the morning, I was given breakfast and taken care of. I never saw a doctor, only the nurses periodically. The nurse gave me intravenously what I needed to get well from the venereal disease, and God gave me spiritually what I needed to heal – time off the streets and an encounter with the Holy Spirit.

I was in the hospital exactly seven days, and the seventh day was Easter Sunday. As Easter Sunday approached, while lying in the hospital, the dawn met my eyes with a glimmer of hope. As the sun continued to rise, the cross on top of the building across from the hospital began to shine through the window directly onto my bed, making a shadowed presentation. God had had enough and was now making His voice heard and known. The voice of the monkey on my back slowly but surely became silent, moment by moment, minute by minute, hour by hour and day by day. God had had enough!

I was able to take a shower every day, sometimes multiple times a day because I was trying to cleanse outwardly what I felt inwardly. That was just what God needed to do for me. He heard my faint and earnest cry, my moans and my groans for Him. When my mind and my words would not form or articulate what my spirit needed, God still heard me. He saw me in the room alone. I was in a single hospital room, and to this date more than 30 years later, I still have not received a bill. God had had enough!

As it was Easter Sunday, I went to the Chapel on the main level. The priest prayed with me, served me Communion, and gave me a Good News Bible, which I devoured. When I got back to my room, I did not want to stay in my room. I began visiting the patients in each room along the corridor of my floor, and I began praying for them. One of the nurses looked at me and said, "You do not look like you need to be here." I replied, "I no longer feel like I need to be here."

The next day was Monday, a new start to a brand-new week. I was discharged in the fashion of a send-off party. I felt good, clean enough to go home to my mom's home, and that's where I went. I was received with love. There was a watchful eye over me, simply out of love. I was so broken, but I appreciated the care which I received. There were many phone calls to my son – moments of silence on the phone and moments of quiet burning tears. I did not know how to explain that I was working towards getting better; all I could do on most calls was listen to him breathe, and for me, that was enough.

The Lord healed my life from crack cocaine and cigarettes. I never looked back, nor did I go back. The Lord gave me such a hatred for that life, and He placed me on a street called "straight." Now the work of healing and mending were beginning. I never experienced any withdrawals. The monkey's voice of crack cocaine was silenced while I was in a place of healing in the hospital. I have not heard that voice since then – glory to God! Peace settled over me in my mom's home during this season. Peace rested upon me like a blanket; it covered me.

I began attending my mom's church. The word of the Lord, the fellowship of the saints, and the work and service of the ministry fed my hunger for community and involvement. My life continued to move towards healing, especially with my son. Although he never returned to a home with me, we continued to talk, communicate, mend our hearts, and commit to grow into a healthy, viable relationship as mother and son. This took years to work through and walk out. Although the healing I experienced in the hospital was immediate deliverance from crack cocaine, the healing of my relationship with my son and the foundational grip of shame that I had to deal with took years to heal.

At the writing of this book, my son is now married with two beautiful children. We are and have been on our healing journey. I write this in transparency so that you can see, in real life, that God may take a situation and completely bring a miracle to it. For others, it is almost like He says, "I will give you the tools to work through it. It will not be easy, but I will be with you." This is what Christ has done for me and my son. Although the Lord has healed me completely from the drug addiction of crack cocaine, He continues to provide to both me and my son the tools to work through the journey of healing from me abandoning him due to my drug addiction. We are working through it, and it makes the journey all the more sweeter when you can learn to love even at a greater measure, when you can learn to trust, to believe in, and to hope with and for one another at a greater measure. Family is worth it, and I am glad that my son knows that I am worth it. I know he, his wife, and my grandchildren are worth it, and so I put the work in. All of us put the work in, and to date, we are still "putting the work in." The reward is a journey of life and love.

Just as the miracle of deliverance took place in my life with the cocaine addiction and the Lord moved His hand and brought about the journey of healing for me and my son, the Holy Spirit still had a work to do regarding the residual effects I was dealing with, namely shame. With my newfound relationship with Christ beginning with so much love and connection, the Holy Spirit wanted more for me. I wanted more for myself, but I had to be slowly introduced to the emotional, mental, and physical work that it would take to walk through the journey of being healed and delivered from the spirit of shame.

Shame prevented me from fully living, loving, and forgiving myself. Even though I looked, lived, and smelled like I was delivered and healed (and I was), deep within my heart shame still resided. Shame collided with the destiny that God had planned for me and began to wrestle with my days and nights, yelling and screaming, "I'm not letting you go… you belong to me." This was my very active imagination, however, it felt like I was being torn and made to remain emotionally and mentally bound by what happened and what I allowed. In life, the unchanging choices and decisions that we make can grip us and be the leverage that shame uses to keep us condemned, broken, head down, and beaten. This was shame attempting to tighten its grip around my throat and stop me from breathing in the fresh air given by the Holy Spirit. I suffered with hurt and so much disappointment due to my own decisions, and shame knew this; shame was aware.

Thankfully, the Lord would woo me into His presence through songs and worship. I would get so caught up in worship that I would lose track of time. I began experiencing relief from the feelings of shame, but shame was not going to go away quietly like the monkey on my back. Shame was putting up a fight. It was a fight that I was unprepared for, and shame knew it. Shame knew that I had cowered down before. It knew my history; however, the Holy Spirit was even more prepared for this fight. Over time, the Holy Spirit equipped me and is still to this day continuing to prepare me for the blows of shame. I still fight with shame. Shame no longer has a hold of my neck. However, its tentacles are long and far reaching; it will release, draw back, and then lash out, seemingly out of nowhere. That is one of shame's best blows.

You see, I know about shame. I know the length, breadth, and width of shame. I know the **subtleness**, the **hatred** that one seeps down into because of shame, the **anger** that one experiences over and over, the seemingly never-ending disappointment in one's self due to shame, and the **memories**, the very vivid memories that haunt you during both the waking and sleeping hours. Yes, I know about shame, but Christ has come to deliver you and me completely from shame. He has taken hold of every voice of shame and has silenced it and brought healing on such a deep level in my life and in the life of my family.

For me, because I had nothing else to offer, I had nothing else to hide or show. All I had was thanksgiving, deep from my heart which poured forth as a child overwhelmed at the love of a parent who had just delivered them from a bad dream; the child was awaken out a dream and was sweating and crying in their sleep, this was me. I was being chased by shame, I was being pursued continuously by a monster of bad choices and bad decisions, and shame shrouded them with a cloak of darkness and came after me. But yet, my Heavenly Father came to my bedside, not my graveside, and took me in His arms and began to whisper to me, "It's ok; you're safe now. I'm here." He shielded me, He protected me, and all I could do was praise and offer my praise with strong crying and tears that would not cease. People would look at me and they would say that it does not take all of that, but they did not know that my Heavenly Father had come to my rescue in the middle of my darkest night and pulled me out of the grips of shame. I will forever praise Him because He saw me on death's hill, sliding down, my fingers gripping the dirt, trying to climb up and out but there was no way out. No one could catch me, nor did they even want to catch me. They could not catch me because they were unaware; but my Father knew. He caught me. Second Corinthians 12:9-10 (NKJV) states, *"And He said to me, 'My grace is sufficient for you, for My strength is made perfect in weakness.' Therefore most gladly I will rather boast in my infirmities, that the power of Christ may rest upon me. Therefore I take pleasure in infirmities, in reproaches, in needs, in persecutions, in distresses, for Christ's sake. For when I am weak, then I am strong."*

    As I was meditating, the Holy Spirit reminded me of the love of God that has been and continues to be poured forth in my life. The love of the Lord our Savior speaks audibly in our lives and is felt so tangibly. It manifests to us that Christ Jesus loves us too much to leave us like He found us. He loves us so very much, even when we feel unlovable, untouchable, and unnoticed. The Lord reminds me that He still loves me. He desires to touch me, and He will always touch me, even when people will not touch me for fear of catching what they think I have. This was the leper's issue, remember? Christ will always see me, and Christ will always see you, friend. Because of His deep and undisturbed love for us, we will never be unnoticed by Him. He will always see us.

    Remember Hagar from Genesis 16 and 21? She remains to be one of my favorite people in the Bible because she was simply doing what she was told to do. Hagar was a slave girl who was Sarai's (Abram's wife) handmaid. Because Sarai could not have children, she gave her handmaid to her husband so that they could have children by her (which was a Biblical custom). When Hagar knew that she had conceived, Sarai became jealous and her rage caused her to mistreat

Hagar so much that Hagar ran away due to the punishment she received from Sarai.

> *Abram replied, "Look, she is your servant, so deal with her as you see fit." Then Sarai treated Hagar so harshly that she finally ran away.*
> *The angel of the LORD found Hagar beside a spring of water in the wilderness, along the road to Shur. The angel said to her, "Hagar, Sarai's servant, where have you come from, and where are you going?"*
> *"I'm running away from my mistress, Sarai," she replied.*
> *The angel of the LORD said to her, "Return to your mistress, and submit to her authority." Then he added, "I will give you more descendants than you can count."*
> *And the angel also said, "You are now pregnant and will give birth to a son. You are to name him Ishmael (which means* **'God hears'**)*, for the LORD has heard your cry of distress. This son of yours will be a wild man, as untamed as a wild donkey! He will raise his fist against everyone, and everyone will be against him. Yes, he will live in open hostility against all his relatives."*
> *Thereafter, Hagar used another name to refer to the LORD, who had spoken to her. She said,* **"You are the God who sees me."** *She also said,* **"Have I truly seen the One who sees me?"** *So that well (the place where water was drawn) was named Beer-lahai-roi (which means "well of the Living One who sees me").*
> - Genesis 16:6-14 (NLT, emphasis mine)

Beloved friend, I say to you as I continue to encourage myself that God sees you. No matter where we are, no matter what we have gone through, He still sees us. He still sees us if for whatever reason we are still carrying our pain. Our discomfort has not gone unnoticed by Him. He is fully aware of where we are, and even before we call, He is primed and positioned to answer.

May I challenge you to place the book down for a moment and simply listen to what the Holy Spirit is saying to you and prompting you to do in this moment? Give in to your heart's plea to our Heavenly Father now and listen for His whispering love to you. You will be transformed in this very moment because you did.

Prayer

Heavenly Father, thank you for promising through Your Word that You will deal with those who assault me, my children, and my grandchildren. Father, shame is continuing to assault me, and I remind you as well as myself that Your Word says that **You will deal with those who assault me**. Father, help me to stand firm in You, not listening to the voices of my past but hearing Your promises for my future. God, I lean into what Your Word says to me, and I remember that I belong to you. I am not a vagabond nor am I an orphan. I belong to You because You sent Your Son Jesus Christ to suffer, bleed, and die for me and purchase my salvation on Calvary's cross. Father, I praise You now for Christ did not remain in a grave; He got up and has risen with all power in His hands. Now Lord God, I plead the Blood of Jesus over my mind, my emotions, my children, my grandchildren, and their destinies. By faith I stand firm and steady on every promise of the Word of God. I do not walk, run, live, or sit in shame, but I walk, run, live, and rule from the place of a victor and not a victim. I am in You, secured in You and in Christ's Name – this is my heritage and the heritage of my family. Amen.

Rejection

The word rejection is difficult to write. Rejection has a few definitions dealing with a person or a thing. According to Merriam-Webster's online dictionary, the definition for the word rejection is: (a) the act of not accepting, believing or considering something; (b) an immune response in which foreign tissue (as of a skin graft or transplanted organ) is attacked by an immune system. The synonyms (alternative words) are: denial, disallowance, negation, disconfirmation, contradiction, denegation, disallowance and disavowal. The antonyms (opposite words) are: acknowledgement, admission, confirmation, avowal.

Just as there is a natural side to life that we see, there is also a spiritual side to life. The spiritual side to life is the opposite, in that it is that which we do not see.

I do not think I heard the word rejection used in a Christian context until approximately the year 2017. It was spoken by two highly respected and recognized deliverance ministers. I had felt rejected, yet I never gave an actual word to what I was feeling. The closest I came to thought processes regarding the word rejection was in elementary school during recess. The kids were forming teams for kick ball or dodge ball. Another girl and I were the last persons chosen, and then it was still with much regret. This was the closest I had come to the description of the word rejection.

But as we know, our adult lives have a way of intensifying our past and present hurts and disappointments. Although this book has taken me more than 30 years to write, this particular layer of my story has taken me the longest. I kept putting it off. Because I would sit at my computer and simply agonize over telling this part of my story which you are about to read. In fact, the entire book was completed and yet I still had this layer on guilt, rejection, and shame to complete. It was extremely hard to write. I kept getting brain fog; it seemed like the words would not come, and when they did come, the rush of all of the pain, feelings, and remembrance of all that took place came with it: the smells, the remembrance of places and of course, the people. But thanks be unto God who causes me to triumph, literally. I had to press through with much prayer, singing, crying, and fasting to bring this layer to completion. This layer and the one thereafter, as you will read, deals with some of the greatest pain that I experienced after my drug addiction and the abandonment of my son. Continue on with me in the layers of my life as I remember, you experience and we both receive healing for our journey.

The Greatest Hurt

During my mid-late thirties and happily after my drug addiction, I began working at a local hospital and attending college, taking a few classes after work. Me and my son's relationship was mending quite well and I desired to continue to move ahead in life and I wanted him to move ahead with me by being proud of me. As I was moving forward and my future continued to appear bright and promising. Things that were in my past were just that – in my past. I had a smile on my face, and it was as though I was peering through a glass that was certainly hopeful. I continued to attend my mom's church, and I got involved in the ministry there with Sunday School and Bible Study. I was growing in my faith, and the fruit of Christ's love and light was manifesting in my life. After work, school, and church, there was not much a young single and newly celibate Christian woman could do. The church I attended did not have a singles ministry, though singles ministries always seemed to be overcrowded with women anyway, so I looked toward safe outside activities I could participate in.

I was attending school hoping to get a degree in psychology, although it was a long way off, but I was hopeful. I would occasionally attend study sessions for school in a relaxed, safe, and enjoyable atmosphere. It was a charged environment. Everyone was on the same wavelength, ambitiously pursuing their future of a college degree. I was glad to be a part of this crowd because we were focused on mainly the same things: our studies, homework, and finally finishing the work which we started in higher education. It was a good crowd; honestly, some were quite driven, and this helped me to stay focused and more accountable.

That environment is where I met him – the person who would give me reason to smell the beautiful fragrance of flowers anew; the person who smiled and captured my heart with his not-so-funny jokes; the person who seemed to fill a seemingly unfillable void in my heart and in my life; the person who caused me to feel the touch of a man and not cringe. We were physically attracted to one another immediately. He was not a drug dealer; he was tall, thin, educated, and suave. But he was not a Christian, and this is where I really should have backed off. However, I tend to be hard-headed and often learn lessons the hard way. Nothing about him set off any warning alarms, so I kept pursuing him as he was certainly pursuing me.

We continued to date without any physical contact, which certainly was a plus, all the more because I was a confessing Christian. He would meet me at class in the evenings, and we would ride the subway home to my new apartment. He would leave at a decent hour, and all seemed well. One night as I was taking the subway home, the Holy Spirit knew where things were headed, and I confess that I did, too. Unfortunately, this is where my stubbornness lifted its defiant head. I felt the wind of the approaching subway train before I heard it coming through the tunnel to my stop, and just as though there was someone standing behind me to my left, I heard the words from the Holy Spirit say, "He's going to hurt you and hurt you badly." I knew immediately who the "he" was that the Holy Spirit was referring to and immediately, I answered, "I don't care; I am tired of being alone." That was definitely a bad answer.

That is just what happened. I was falling in love with him, and the Holy Spirit knew it. The Holy Spirit gave the warning to me. My job, should I choose to accept it, was to receive the warning and dislodge from him and the relationship immediately. It is not a question as to if I believed Holy Spirit; I completely believed Him, which was evident in my response. I was at a point where if I had ended the relationship, it would have been me adhering to the Holy Spirit and choosing Him due to my love for my Savior. It would have been a sacrifice to leave the relationship and true obedience which the Holy Spirit is looking for; but because I chose my flesh over the Savior of my soul, I had some severe suffering ahead of me, and the Holy Spirit was merely trying to spare me of this.

If we would truly be obedient when the Holy Spirit gives us the opportunity to do so, even if that obedience means a sacrifice on our part, we would be all the better for it. Our life and our destiny would be all the better for it; however, God still uses our mishaps, our mistakes, and our bad choices. He never gives a timestamp on how long it will take. He assures us that He will use them – the good, bad, indifferent and the ugly – *"...work together for good to those who love God, to those who are the called according to His purposes."* Romans 8:28 (NKJV).

One of the main things that I have learned to love more and more about my Heavenly Father is that He is so very patient. He is longsuffering towards His people and His love endures forever. In fact, 2 Peter 3:9 (NLT) says, *"The Lord isn't really being slow about his promise, as some people think. No, he is being patient for your sake. He does not want anyone to be destroyed, but wants everyone to repent."* In the process of time, in the journeys of life, in turning our eyes to Him, and through His patience and enduring love, we learn obedience through the things we suffer. According to Hebrews 5:8 (NLT): *"Even though Jesus was God's Son, he learned obedience from the things he suffered."* We, too, learn obedience from the things we suffer.

I had a lot of learning to do, and the suffering that was about to enter my life through the avenue of love and my own disobedience would bring about obedience much later in my life. But I thank God that in this current season of my life, I am able to enjoy the presence of the Lord, having gone through much suffering and learning obedience through the Word of God and the impressions of the Holy Spirit. I am a little bit more obedient now than I was then. Hear me: I have definitely not arrived. But I have learned the hard way, and now, I am on my way. A hard head really did make a soft resting place.

    I managed to continue to date the young man, and we grew closer in our dating, our connecting, and our time spent together increased as well. I grew to love him like cold water on a hot day. I remember one of my co-workers looking at me after I arrived for work one morning. After getting off the elevator, she looked at me and said, "You have a boyfriend, don't you?"

I said, "Yeah; how can you tell?"

She said, "It's written all over your face: I'm in love."

Surely, I was in love. If I am being truthful, this love brought me to a place where I did not forget God's love for me, but in the moment, my needs and my wants outweighed His love. My feelings, the satisfaction of my will, my needs, and my desires overpowered my remembrance of what He had brought me through more than 10 years before. I was so caught up with how this guy made me feel and how I felt being with him, around him, and lying next to him that I did not take a step back. Christ had set me free; I was assured of this fact. That was a solid deal in my life, and thankfully, my deliverance was sealed and complete.

However, the Holy Spirit will not go against your will. If you desire to walk away and not remember the goodness of the Lord and if you desire to return back to your old ways or go into a new way, it is your choice. However, there are repercussions for disobedience. For me, those repercussions were just what the Holy Spirit said: "He is going to hurt you and hurt you badly."

It took almost two years for that word to come to pass in my life, but the Holy Spirit has never lied. He was extending great mercy and great grace and calling me with dreams and the wooing of His presence, but my flesh held me back. It was not long before I began to put two and two together and realized that when I abandoned my son, it was because of my flesh; now, I was abandoning my belief in God because of my flesh. Why not just marry him? I am glad that never happened. Although he was a good and decent guy, he was a womanizer, though I would find this out much later. I was too much in love to see the forest for the trees, although it was apparent then. There were blazing red flags, but I was caught up in him and always second-guessing myself. I had my flesh to contend with, and during that time, my flesh always won the argument or fight.

Two years into our relationship, my sister married the love of her life. At the wedding reception, I was eating some cherries. I love cherries. I love to put several in my mouth and munch on them, picking out the seeds. Unknowingly, one seed remained in my mouth while I was munching on those cherries. All of a sudden, I had a horrible and painful crunch in the back of my mouth. I inadvertently bit down on a cherry seed and broke a back tooth. I got home later that evening and took some Tylenol for the pain and called it a night. Three days later, my face began to be inflamed and swollen, and I thought something had bit me in the night. Since I worked at a local hospital, during my lunch hour, I went to the emergency room. They examined me and informed me that I needed to see an oral surgeon. I received a referral and made an emergency appointment for the next day. The surgeon told me that the tooth had abscessed, and I needed to have it surgically removed. He could perform the procedure but not until I had received a round of antibiotics, specifically Penicillin, at a high dose to clear all of the infection. He asked the question, "Are you sexually active?" He asked this question because he needed to know if I was taking oral contraceptives. In order to be fully protected against pregnancy, I would need to use a second source of contraception other than birth control pills, if I were to take the round of Penicillin. He explained himself clearly. I heard him correctly; there were no questions. However, I do not know to this day why I lied, but I did. I sat straight in that chair and told a bald-faced lie. I was a consenting adult and all he wanted to know was the truth – he had no jail to put me in; he simply needed to know if I was taking any form of contraception to protect me from becoming pregnant once I began the round of Penicillin, and I lied. Perhaps I thought that I was skirting the truth to God in this authority figure. I lied: "No, I'm not sexually involved." I had the prescription filled, began taking the antibiotics, and eight days later, I had the problem tooth removed.

It was perhaps a couple of months later that I discovered I was pregnant. I could not lie about this. I had told myself and made myself believe that the young man loved me just as I loved him, and me telling him I was pregnant would not be a problem. I loved him, and I knew that we could make it work. I knew that he liked us together. I believed he loved me, but I also knew that I loved him more. I set up a nice romantic atmosphere where I would tell him that I was pregnant. The scene was set, and we were both gleaming with smiles, enjoying one another's presence, then I made a move that I will never forget. I placed his hand on my belly and I said to him, "I am pregnant." He looked at me like I had three heads and then began crying.

I really imagined that going a whole different way. I did not know what to do. I had never seen a man cry in front of me before. In all my immaturity and sincerity, I believed, just for a moment, that these were tears of joy; but the tears were tears of disappointment and anger. I had never seen anyone so angry that they burst into tears. He said to me, "I want you, but I don't want to be a father again."

Again? I thought to myself while taking all of this in. Again? I did not understand. Right then and there, the lies began to unfold. He already had a child by another woman six years before me, but he had kept this a secret. Unfortunately, this discovery also opened the door to more lies of other women that he had been seeing that I was totally unaware of.

We agreed to stop seeing one another, but I went on with the pregnancy. Having an abortion never entered into my mind nor my heart. I was in a great job. I had a nice apartment, and I was doing well in school. I thought to myself that I could do this, and that is just what

I did. I continued on with the pregnancy, but I was not ready for the emotional and mental rejection I would experience. I loved him passionately and although I was pregnant, he had deserted me in the time that I needed him most. Because of us knowing and traveling in some of the same circles, we would occasionally run into one another. He would see my growing baby bump and he would try to connect. But as difficult as it was, I continued to try to move on.

However, during my seventh month of the pregnancy, we reconnected. I tried to look past the previous 6 months and move forward with him instead of being alone. My faith that I could do it alone was waning, and fear was rising. I began seeing him again. This was a time in the pregnancy where one looks beautiful and the backaches and swelling of the feet are not at the forefront, but one is actually enjoying the pregnancy. I was that person. I so enjoyed being pregnant. I would often talk to my daughter while she was in my womb. I would reassure her as I was trying to reassure myself that we would be alright. I often assured her that my love for her and my joy of her presence in my womb and in my life was a beautiful thing, and I was so grateful for the privilege of being her mommy. During such times of bonding, even in the womb, she would respond with nudges of a knee, a kick of her foot, or perhaps the move of an elbow or the brushing of her head or hand. But what encouraged me was that she always responded to my loving affirmations of her and her presence in my life. I enjoyed carrying my daughter in my womb. It was not long after that the young man and I began seeing one another again that it was time to begin Lamaze classes. I was surprised when he wanted to participate and actually showed up to do so. This encouraged my heart as it appeared that he had made the adjustment within himself, and we were definitely moving forward.

I found myself continuing to try hard to make it work with him; and truth be told, he too appeared to be trying hard to make the relationship work. Yet although we were physically together, there was still a void in my soul – a void of missing my son, my baby. It was a void in my heart for my son and a void in my spirit from my relationship with Christ that I was no longer pursuing. There was this unfillable yet tangible empty space, and it seemed to me that I was always trying to fill but it could never be filled, at least not by human touch. Try as we might, we do try to fill the voids in our lives with the human touch, alcohol, drugs, money, and satisfactions of one thing to the next, but after the pleasure is gone, the internal yearning returns and it rises like a midst in the early morning.

Psalm 42:1-2 (NLT) says: *"As the deer longs for streams of water, so I long for you, O God. I thirst for God, the living God. When can I go and stand before him?"* The longing I had was what continued to draw me and woo me into His loving presence, even though I had made mistake after mistake, bad choice after bad choice, and I had continued to ultimately choose my flesh over my relationship with Christ. No matter how that looked, be it choosing drugs, choosing alcohol, choosing a relationship or friendship that ultimately was not His perfect will for my life, ultimately not choosing Christ's best nor His will for our lives is of great concern to Him.

Even in the midst of this, the Holy Spirit kept drawing me. Glory to God! He kept pursuing me. He kept whispering and calling out to me, even though I felt like I was a lost cause; I felt like no one could or would help me. I would just go my own way in my own will. Yet Christ, my loving Savior, continued to chase after me in my dreams, in the middle of the night, in the crack house, even in the loss of the emotions of my own feelings. He pursued me. He continued to pursue me, to look at me with eyes of love to say, "I see you and I want you to experience the love I have for you. When you are ready, come; I will be here waiting." Beloved, I say to you, Christ is waiting to embrace you with open and loving arms to surround you fully. His arms are wide enough to hold you and all of your mishaps, your low self-esteem, your hurt, and your disappointments. His shoulders are wide enough to carry your pain and release you from it, but you have to make the choice to release it and give it to Him. If you feel like you need more time, Christ is there when you are ready.

During the last months of my pregnancy, I found myself lying next to my baby's father in the middle of the night weeping due to my internal yearnings for my son and for Christ. I found myself being awakened out of my sleep. Dreams of my son, his smiling eyes looking at me with a call all their own, would arouse me. I would get up out of the bed and go to another room while weeping and crying. I thought there was nothing I could do. There was nothing that I knew to do. I was missing my relationship with God. Conviction had stormed my gates, and here I was in the middle of the night surrounded by everything that called me into a life of disobedience, and yet Jesus never gave up on me. It was through the dreams that He was wooing me. He was wooing me into His presence. Christ knew my heart for my son, and He was drawing me to Him so that full reconciliation with my son could be realized. Christ was reintroducing my heart to the smile of my son as we were working towards reconciliation, though full restoration and reconciliation were not yet complete between us.

The Lord is so faithful. He was hearing the yearnings of my son who was 10 years old at that time, and He was hearing my cry as well. Christ knew that deep inside of my heart, no satisfaction of my flesh could compare to the soul satisfaction that my son brought me, the spiritual satisfaction that the Holy Spirit brought to me, and the relational satisfaction that the connection and the smile of my son brought me.

While I was overcome with my weeping, here I was in the house of my sinful relationship pouring my heart out before the Lord but not saying anything. My heart was lost for words. What do you say when you do not know what to say? My tears and my weeping became my heart's cry before the Lord, and my spirit began to cry out to the Lord for things I did not know that I needed, just as Romans 8:26 (NLT) says, *"And the Holy Spirit helps us in our weakness. For example, we don't know what God wants us to pray for. But the Holy Spirit prays for us with groanings that cannot be expressed in words."* God answered, and yet the answer did not come in a day, a week, nor a month. It was an answer that took time. As the father of my unborn child reached over in the bed and discovered I was not there, he began calling for me, "Lisa? Lisa, are you here?" Sometimes after these brief encounters of weeping and crying out to God, times of me simply weeping at the feet of Jesus, not asking for one thing, not saying anything, just weeping, I would not answer him when he would call. Finally, after I would not answer, he would get up and come looking for me in the house. When he would find me, he would say, "Did you not hear me calling you?" I would answer "I heard you calling me, but I was answering another call." He would see my tears, and he would go back to bed. He would not say anything. He would just leave the room and go back to bed, and I eventually went back to bed, too.

It was not long after that I was ready to delivery my second bundle of joy. I thought that because we had completed the Lamaze classes together that he would be there. I thought that since we were attempting to make things work, as hard as they were, he would be there. Yet, when I went into labor, I was at work, and I left my office to walk across the street to the hospital. I was prepped in labor and delivery, and I was ready to deliver my daughter, my precious baby girl. My doctor, who was also my supervisor, said, "I will go and call the baby's dad and let him know that you are approaching active delivery. If he is coming, now is the time to get here."

She did what she said. She called, and he answered. She let him know that I was approaching active delivery, the stage where I would begin pushing. She asked him if he would be coming. He told her that he would not be coming. She came back and looked at me; she was not only my physician but also my friend. She looked at me and I looked at her, through the sweat and tears. I knew he was not coming. I had no idea the conversation they had, but I knew he was not coming. By that time, I had certainly learned enough about him to come to the conclusion that he was not coming.

When she shook her head no, I asked, "Did you call him?"
She said, "Yes, I did."
I responded, "Was he there; did he answer the phone?"

She said, "Yes, he did."

I said, "Is he coming?"

Again, she said, "No, he's not."

At that moment everything stopped. I stopped breathing. I stopped hearing. I stopped listening and more importantly, I stopped pushing. Everything stopped. Finally, she realized she needed to deliver my baby girl by forceps. She performed her job, even though I had given up on mine. She took me and held me close to her heart as I cried my way through a moment that was supposed to be full of joy, bonding, and connectivity. She held me through it all while the associate doctor delivered my daughter via forceps. She whispered, "You are strong, and you will be alright."

At home with my mom and family in the comfort and protection of my mom's home, family visited us often. The house seemed to be alive with food, family, laughter, and loud talking of those who came by to wish me and my daughter well. Everything was right and everything was well.

Four weeks later, I went back home to my apartment. I continued to enjoy the new life with my daughter. Things were quiet, and we were in need of nothing. Once I was back to work, I had developed a system of working, transporting my baby to and from daycare, commuting for work, cooking, bath time, and feeding. The fear of raising my daughter was dissipating. I was managing. I was doing okay. Reconciliation was happening for my son and me, and he enjoyed his sister. Things were working, and I was happy about it. I was no longer having dreams of my son; he was in our lives, visiting with me and my daughter, his sister. I was no longer weeping and crying, but I was experiencing times of laughter and sheer joy at seeing my kids play together, them enjoying one another and me enjoying them, and my mom and family enjoying us all when we would visit. We were a family.

My daughter's father did not come to see her until 3 months after her birth. There were no arguments. There were no ultimatums given. When he did finally show up, we greeted one another, and he was able to embrace and hold his daughter for the first time. I gave him space to enjoy her, and truthfully, it was good to see him interact with her, even in a brief way. My longing for my own father visited my heart and mind, so I was more generous with him visiting and not fussing at him. After all, truth be told, I still loved this man. As broken and as disconnected as we were, I still loved him. Even though there was a wall between us now, which was clearly visible to me, even if not to him. When I had times alone, I would argue with myself that no one would put up with what I had put up with. But this is untrue. In fact, there are more women and men who have put up with, dealt with, and have nursed these types of co-dependent relationships as long as relationships have existed. Some hide it very well and condemn others while they are hiding theirs.

We continued with brief visits and over a period of time, I noticed him inserting himself back into our lives. I realized that he was calling more, asking to come by more, and appearing to be more concerned if we needed anything. Unfortunately, this apparent caring mechanism was short-lived, but it was enough to get him back in the door. We tried to make it work for more than 18 months. We both tried to build our trust for one another, tear down old thoughts, occurrences, reoccurrences, and bad memories, and start our relationship anew. But after many arguments, slammed doors, and times of disappearances, it was clear that we could not make it work. The make-ups became few and far between the arguments and the break-ups.

How do you make something work when it was never meant to work? How do you keep trying when your life is ordained by God for destiny and the other person's life is destined for the opposite direction of yours? The answer is that we stop trying to make something work when God never intended for it to work. But keep in mind, the Holy Spirit will not go against our human will. He does not push His way with an audacious move. That is not the Holy Spirit; that is Satan at his best. Satan attempts to manipulate and deceive to get his way, at all costs. That's not love's way. The Holy Spirit is

Love, and He ultimately works for the good of the children of God and for their destiny called forth from the beginning of time. Sometimes, through our disobedience, our situations, and our circumstances, we make His job so complicated, but in the end, He still gets the greater glory for the work which seemed to you and I to have been impossible. From it, we see a mature life beaming with God's richness, mercy, and glory.

In a moment of time, I was able to look at myself and see what no one else could see, at least not my daughter's and my soon-to-be youngest son's father. Eighteen months had passed with us trying, stopping, beginning again, and getting frustrated, only for us to do it all over again. At a yearly physical examination, I looked at my doctor with tears crisscrossing underneath my chin and said, "I feel like I'm pregnant."

She turned beet red; she remembered my horrendous disappointment 18 months ago with the father of my daughter. Surely, we are not about to replay this entire movie again. She did not say this; she is a professional. But if a screen could reveal her heart, this is what she was thinking. She stepped towards me to catch me in her arms as I released my pain and frustration at myself. She drew blood from my arm herself. She could have called in her assistant to take care of that, but she handled me with such care by doing everything herself.

She called me the next day herself. She walked with me through the entire nine months of this precious pregnancy of my youngest son. She fell in love with us both – me and my growing tummy. She adopted me as a dear friend all over again, even though she was my supervisor at work and my obstetrician/gynecologist. I endured the entire pregnancy alone except for my loving family and friends, my sister, my dearest girlfriend, and my doctor-friend.

During this pregnancy, as with my daughter's pregnancy, I asked the Lord what I should name my baby. I felt deeply in my heart to name him a Hebrew name which meant faithful, whole-hearted, bold, and brave. Truly, it was my desire that he would grow up to exemplify the heart-felt meaning of his name. My pregnancy with him was surrounded with peace.

At the time of delivery, we never called his father; I didn't want to give him a chance to deny me or his son his presence as he had did with his daughter. I was fully engaged in this delivery, and I wanted to stay that way. With my best friends, my doctor and my son's godmother, we breathed, pushed, and delivered a beautiful and strong baby boy. My youngest son went home with me the next day and he, my daughter, and I melted into the love of family. We grew together. He is part of the joy that I share with my oldest son and my daughter. During his infancy, he would nurse and sleep well, cuddled up next to me. I would watch him sleep for hours during the night while I was home on maternity leave. My daughter and I would play with him, counting fingers and toes, planting whispers of kisses on his neck, and holding him close until it seemed like they both melted in my embrace. I enjoyed being a mom – their mom.

But I was doing it alone. This was scary. As the time approached for me to go back to work, the enemy would visit with his threats, "What are you going to do?" "How is this going to work out?" I did not have the answers. I could not pretend. In fact, I was tired of pretending. I stopped trying to answer him; I stopped trying to answer myself. I just kept getting up in the morning, taking care of my family, and going to sleep in the evening. At that time, that was all I could do.

My daughter and son's father came to see his children. He was welcomed by me and his kids. We fed and bathed the children and put them to bed. He was quiet and so was I. He later asked me why I did not let him know that I was in the hospital delivering our son. I simply stared at him. I reminded myself that up until that time, things in the home were peaceful, mainly because there was no one to argue with. I took a slow, long, deep breath and softly reminded him that I simply did not want to be disappointed again. He offered his apology for bringing unnecessary strain and stress upon me and to our relationship, or the lack thereof. Surprisingly, he left that evening without a confrontation. But he began, once again, inserting himself into our lives. Looking at all that I was facing, I welcomed him being more visible in my home and being involved in our children's lives. I never realized it until the writing of this book that he was just as broken as I was, if not more. I am sure he would never admit it, but he continued to return to the normalcy of life and love, which is what I represented to him because everything else in his life came up short of that.

During those weeks of postpartum care, he was there, helping where help was needed. Although we did not argue, fuss, nor fight, his presence was welcomed. Even without having to return to work due to being on maternity leave, it was still hard raising and caring for a 2 year old and a newborn. We were able to talk through a lot of our issues, though later I realized that he never meant a word of what he was saying and promising. He told his mom about me and the kids, and we appeared to be a couple on the outside among our friends. But as genuine as we could be on the outside, behind closed doors, we were back at it, trying to make something work that was not working. He provided presence and nothing else. He was there, but being a father requires you to be more than "there." I had to learn this. I also had to learn that it is better to be alone and move forward than to pull and tug someone else who really does not want to go where you are going, no matter how much they try to convince you that they are on board. This is what my children's dad attempted to do; he tried to convince me that he was on board. But I knew better; I knew it wasn't his heart, and his actions betrayed him time and time again. But I am hard-headed, and I kept trying. I thought my love would be enough to keep him and silence my fears, but only Christ's love can keep a soul from wandering and silence the enemy's voice in both our hearts and in our minds. Unfortunately, one painful part remained – I still loved him, and I gave into that love even to feel his embrace.

We try and we convince ourselves that he will not hit us again. We try and convince ourselves that the other women really do not matter to him. We try and convince ourselves of the lie time and time again, but the truth always stands up straight, tall, and without a chaser and says, "I am here and you cannot deny me." In the weeks to come, truth finally took a stand. Whether I wanted to admit it or be in agreement with it or not, truth was unfolding and there was nothing I could do to stop it. I allowed his warm embrace to comfort me, not realizing that this last time was a very heavy price to continue to pay for both my reluctance and my disobedience. But as it would turn out, it was the final time. Unfortunately, the life of the baby that I could not keep in my womb was enough for me to finally say, both to myself and for myself, "Enough is enough."

Guilt

According to Merriam-Webster.com, abort[8] means to bring forth stillborn, nonviable, or premature offspring; to terminate a procedure prematurely; to interrupt or stop; "1. To induce the abortion of or give birth to prematurely; 1b: to terminate the pregnancy of before term. 2. To stop in the early stages (such as) abort a disease."

I remember going back for my six-week check-up after my son was born and being told that I was pregnant. It was like my whole being shut down. I knew I did not have the fortitude to go through another pregnancy alone or to endure the arguments, the snide remarks, or even the silence. I knew what I had to do; I felt like I had no other choice. I made the appointment. While I laid on the sterile table, in a silent room with my thoughts, angels and demons were at war. At one point, I felt I was disconnected from my body, and I was watching what was going on because my mind and heart could not take what my will was allowing to happen. I did not stop it; I could not stop it. I could hear the arguments: "How are you going to feed this child?" "How are you going to pay for a babysitter?" "What about daycare?" "What about milk and diapers?" The final question, the one

---

[8] https://www.merriam-webster.com/dictionary/abort

that stung the most was, "How could you let this happen... again, multiplied by 3?" I was lost in the questions that were coming much too fast.

My heart did not stop, but its beat became silent within me. As the doctor and nurse administered pain blockers, numbness began to slowly creep up my legs and take hold of my pelvis. I seeped into a place between there and nowhere. For me, it was a place where the sounds in the room became muffled, and all I could hear were the clamping of the steel, hardened instruments peering through the innermost part of my body, to the place where it was supposed to have been the safest place in the world for my baby. Somehow, I had to come to grips with what I was allowing in order for me to get myself together, get off the table, put my clothes and shoes back on, get my purse, and walk out of that doctor's office as though I was another stable human being. I walked across the street to take the bus to the nearest Metro station, and while I was waiting for the bus to come, it felt like my senses were returning to me, one sense at a time. I finally got to the point where I could feel the air on my skin; visually, things were coming into focus. It is not funny at all when you are in an extremely tight place with life and your body and mind goes on automatic. I had to keep going. I could not stop. At one point, I noticed that I had not tied my shoes correctly, I mumbled to myself, "Bend down and tie your shoes, the bus is about to come." I had to keep it together and make my way to the daycare center to pick up my daughter and then to the babysitter to pick up my son who were waiting for me, because their world had continued to spin as normal, although mine had come to an abrupt halt.

As I have shared so many private and transparent moments of my life, please know that I am doing so to be a witness that healing is available to you also, not just for me and for "others." I bring up this point because when we read about healing, deliverance, and miracles, we often believe and accept it for that person that we are reading about and not for ourselves. Sometimes if we do believe and accept it for ourselves, we do not continue and remain in that place until we see the manifestation of the healing, the deliverance, and the miracle.

What about not just physical healing, what about in emotional areas of deliverance such as deliverance from guilt? To have the cloud of guilt finally removed from our present, removed from our future, and once and for all removed from our destiny, our lives – this is possible not just for me and others, this is possible for you! In life, we have done things and made decisions that have gripped our very being, and we look and we say to ourselves, "I'm done." We say what the enemy is repeating over and over in our head: "You're done, you're guilty, and there is no other way that you can ever live this down." I say to you with my loudest outside voice, "IT'S NOT OVER FOR YOU! You do not have to carry guilt to the grave!"

You do not have to carry the weight of the decisions which you made in your past, whether informed or non-informed decisions, good or bad decisions. With Christ, you do not have to bear the burden alone! I realize that there are repercussions for mistakes and decisions made. I fully agree, and even in the repercussions, Christ is with you. Christ is with us to help us so that we are not alone shouldering the weight of those repercussions. Yes, I did it, but Christ helps me through it! Yes, I made the mistake, but Christ helps me through it and teaches me and guides me to better decisions and better choices. You said it and you may have done it; however, you are not the mistake you made nor are you the bad decision you made.

Isaiah 53:6 (NKJV) says, *"All we like sheep have gone astray; We have turned, every one, to his own way; And the LORD has laid on Him the iniquity of us all."* Also, Romans 3:23 (NKJV) says, *"For all have sinned and fall short of the glory of God."* Friend, we are not perfect. However, Christ is perfect; He is the spotless Lamb of God who shed His blood on the cross for all humanity.

First John 1:9-10 (NKJV) says, *"If we confess our sins, He is faithful and just to forgive us of our sins and to cleanse us from all unrighteousness. If we say we have not sinned, we make Him a liar, and His word is not in us."* I believe verse 10 speaks volumes for us, especially in the culture which we live. It says, clearly, *"If we say we have not sinned, we make Him a liar..."* We are often not willing to say that we have sinned. We are not willing to be honest and admit our wrongs. Often, especially with regards to guilt, we get so caught up in the lie that we no longer know where the truth is. Friend, the truth is in confessing the wrong; it does not matter who is at fault. Do not play the blame game with God. Own up to the part you played in the situation. I have found that the moment I confess my wrong to Christ, my shoulders go limp. I find that I am no longer trying to hold up and stand strong under the load of guilt once I have surrendered and confessed my heart to Christ. Christ's light begins to pierce my darkness, and it almost feels as though I can finally lay my head on His shoulder and experience His rest.

In meditating further in this truth, I believe the Lord impressed upon my heart the story of the prodigal son in Luke 15. I reread the story for myself; now, please allow the Holy Spirit to minister the story to your heart. In Luke 15:11-24, we don't just read the story of the prodigal son but we experience it. In summary, a father had two sons. The younger son did not ask but told the father to give to him the portion of goods that he would inherit. The father did so and divided his goods to both sons. The younger son took his share, journeyed to a far country, and wasted all of his possessions with riotous (unruly, uncontrollable, lawless) living. However, when he had wasted everything he had, there arose a famine and he began to be in need. He went to work for a man who sent him into the fields to feed the pigs on his property. The prodigal son would have gladly eaten the pods that the pigs ate because no one was giving him anything.

Now, there is so much in the above summary; however, let's zoom in what I believe the Holy Spirit is making relevant to us in this hour. It says in verse 17 (NKJV), *"But when he came to himself he said, how many of my father's hired servants have bread enough and to spare, and I perish with hunger!"* I had to have a "come to myself" moment, and you are destined for a "come to yourself" moment also.

What is a "come to yourself" moment? It is when you wake up, the blinders are finally off of your eyes and your mind, and you realize that you are in a place where you should not be. When you come to yourself, you realize that things were not so bad after all; you realize how good you had it. When you come to yourself, you **Recognize, Repent, Return,** and **Receive**. The Scripture says that after the son came to himself, he said to himself, *"I will arise and go to my father, and will say to him, Father I have sinned against heaven and before you and I am no longer worthy to be called your son. Make me like one of your hired servants"* (verses 18-19, NKJV). Sometimes, we feel so broken down with guilt, that we think of ourselves and to ourselves, "I am not worthy to be owned as your son or daughter; make me one of your servants. I will work for you. I will serve you. I no longer deserve the rights of an heir, the love of communicating with the father and the touch that comes from the father to a child."

Guilt attempts to strip away all the beauty of the love of a father to a son or daughter. Guilt tells us that we do not belong because the thing that we did made us unworthy to be a part of the family. Perhaps guilt said to you that the abortion you had made you unworthy to be called a daughter. Perhaps guilt told you that because you left the church, you are no longer called a son. Maybe guilt says to you that because you cannot seem to stop drinking, you have no place in the family. Maybe you have listened to guilt so long from a prison cell, and guilt keeps reminding you of the murder you committed; you became angry, started a fight, and the bullet pierced a child's heart and not its intended target. You are angry, bitterly angry, yet you weep in the middle of the night, and you are overwhelmed with guilt. I say to you, no amount of guilt will ever keep you from the Father's love! The Father's love cannot be suppressed by guilt! The Father's love and covering cannot be dismissed, erased, nor eradicated. He loves YOU. He loves me. The Father's love for you and me is eternal!

Luke 15:20 (NKJV) says, *"And he arose and came to his father. But when he was still a great way off, his father saw him and had compassion and ran and fell on his neck and kissed him."* Listen to the son as he repents before his father: *"And the son said to him, 'Father, I have sinned against heaven and in your sight, and am no longer worthy to be called your son'"* (verse 21, NKJV). But the father's response is: *"But the father said to his servants, 'Bring out the best robe and put it on him and put a ring on his hand and sandals on his feet. Bring the fatted calf here and kill it and let us eat and be merry; for my son was dead and is alive again; he was lost and is found. And they began to be merry"* (verses 22-24, NKJV).

You, beloved, may be mentally or in your heart "a great way off." You may not be one hundred percent sure; you may still feel "a great way off" but you are on the path to the Father's house. You are on the path home! The Father sees you! We may have wasted all that was given into our hands; we may have wasted dreams, finances, relationships, responsibilities, and one of the more important commodities of our season: time. But our Father is the redeemer of all things, and it is not over!

Get up and **Recognize, Repent,** and **Return**. When the father saw him, he told the servants to bring out the best robe, the Father's robe of righteousness; disrobe from the guilt, remove the guilt, and put on the Father's robe of righteousness! **Recognize, Repent, Return,** and **Receive**! Get up, **Recognize, Repent, Return** to the Father, and **Receive** the righteousness that the Father is wanting to wrap you in. Beloved, put on the robe of righteousness and allow the Father to place the ring of belonging (identity) on your finger and the shoes on your feet. You no longer have to feel guilty nor be in a place of barren emptiness due to all that you have lost. You, friend, are free, and the Father loves and receives you. Receive all that He has for you.

Isaiah 61 speaks of the good news of salvation. Specifically, verse 10 (NKJV) says, *"I will greatly rejoice in the Lord, my soul shall be joyful in my God; for He has clothed me with the garments of salvation, He has covered me with the robe of righteousness, as a bridegroom decks himself with ornaments, and as a bride adorns herself with her jewels."* Once you **Recognize, Repent,** and **Return,** be sure to **Receive** what is rightfully yours – the robe of righteousness!

Look at the analogy that Scripture provides, "as a bridegroom decks himself… and as a bride adorns herself." The robe of righteousness is a beautiful garment in the spirit, and only an heir can be clothed in it. Righteousness and right standing awaits you, beloved – you are no longer guilty!

Layer Seven ~ FEAR

Did you grow up in an atmosphere of fear where there was always something lurking around you or over you? It could have all been in your mind, but it was tangibly real to you. You are not alone in this thought process. Others have related that feeling of something lurking around and/or over them to the fear of foreboding, believing that if something bad was going to happen, it would happen to you and it would happen sooner rather than later. Fear causes us to make mistakes that normally we would not make, if we were not fearful or did not have the handicap of fear.

Unfortunately, some may have been raised in an environment where hesitancy, apprehension, second guessing, or a list of other uncertainties was the norm of the day. Perhaps your parents or guardians would not allow you to step out and spread your wings because they may have been fearful of you doing something that would cause you to hurt yourself, fearful of what might happen to you should you hurt yourself, or fearful of what you would get involved in. But when you have nothing else to lose, you walk away from fear, and you do it afraid. We do that until we learn how to do it courageously, and that is what I have become an advocate of: courageously living my life and breaking up with fear, intimidation, trepidation, and all of the other scenarios that surround hesitancy and procrastination to moving forward in life, love, business, relationships, ministry, and the Kingdom of God.

This book is more than 30 years old, even though it was not published until 2021. This book consists of my life experiences, true to form, with all of its transparencies. As I seriously contemplated writing this book, I asked God, "Do you know what people would think and say about me if I write this book, with all of its intricate details of my life, written for the world to see?" Over and over again, the Lord made it absolutely clear that I was to write the book withholding nothing. Sometimes I wrote through tears from revisiting moments, episodes, and memories of shame and rejection, and I had bouts of fear. Yet I had to write this book because all that I have been through and continue to go through may release someone, even just one person, from the grips of shame, rejection, guilt, fear, and Satan himself. To God be all of the glory for all of it!

In writing this book, I had to confront many of my fears. One of my fears that had dominated my life and even tried to control my ministry was the fear of man. This fear developed and showed up as: "What would she think?" "What would he think?" "What would they think?" "Did I say that wrong?" "Did I do enough research or work?" Sometimes, the fear of man shows up as wanting approval, trying to please others, and going overboard in order to do so.

I shared a story in an earlier Layer from one of the gentleman that I worked for. He said to me, "You would work yourself to death, if I let you." Do you have this need to feel validated, appreciated, and/or please people? These are the world's terms, but Scripture refers to this as the fear of man. Proverbs 29:25 (NKJV) says, *"The fear of man brings a snare, but whoever trusts in the Lord shall be safe."* The word for fear in the Hebrew is "chărâdâh" and the word also means extreme anxiety, quaking, anxious care, and trembling. This type of fear is crippling. The Lord does not wish that His child, His beloved, would live his/her life in this state.

This type of fear, the fear of man, ultimately cripples your thought processes so that you end up second guessing yourself in your responses, in your work, and in every area of life. You second guess yourself to the point that you are unsure of all your comings and your goings. You become intimidated by others who are merely rising up in their own authenticity; in them being themselves, you feel less of yourself. Jealousies arise in situations such as this because you desperately want to be who you were created to be and do what you were created to do, but you have this fear that is preventing you, intimidating you, and halting you at every turn. That fear is the fear of man. It is controlling the narrative of your life, and it is preventing you from living. Life becomes stagnant for you; you may feel like you are walking with cement in your shoes, your hands are not productive, and that everyone else is far surpassing you. This is part of the trap that the enemy of our souls has for the life of every human being.

A part of the enemy's plan is just as Proverbs 29:25 states: *"The fear of man is a snare."* The word snare[9] is also translated in some versions as a trap, a lure, a noose (for catching animals, literally or figuratively), or a hook (for the nose). This wider definition brings even more clarity of this word "snare." The enemy has plans for our lives, just as our heavenly Father has plans for our lives; however, Satan's plans are perverted.

The Lord God says in Jeremiah 29:11 (NLT), *"'For I know the plans I have for you,' says the Lord. 'They are plans for good and not for disaster, to give you a future and a hope.'"* Beloved, God has plans for your life, and those plans do not include you being afraid of man so that you no longer live free. Walk in the fear of God and His plans and purposes for your life and your destiny. God ordained that in light of our life experiences, we would rise from the ashes which surrounded our lives and write, preach, sing, dance, operate businesses, raise families, build buildings, administrate, pastor, teach, prophesy, heal the sick, raise the dead, and perform other miracles as He desires. He wants you and me to be richly involved in life, not afraid to live. Stop being afraid to live! I have to tell myself this more than just once. Stop being afraid to live! No longer be afraid of who God made you to be. If you sincerely do not know who that is, who you are, this is one of the most profound discoveries that you will ever

---

[9] https://www.google.com/search?q=snare&rlz=1C1GCEV_enUS893US897&oq=snare&aqs=chrome..6 9i57j69i61.1311j0j15&sourceid=chrome&ie=UTF-8

make in life. As it has been said by many pastors, coaches, and mentors quoting from Mark Twain, "The two most important days in your life are the day you were born and the day you find out why!"

Jeremiah 1:5a (NKJV) says, *"Before I formed you in the womb I knew you, and before you were born I sanctified you."* Ephesians 1:4 (NLT) says, *"Even before he made the world, God loved us and chose us in Christ to be holy and without fault in his eyes."* Beloved, the Lord God chose you before you were formed in your momma's womb. Before the time would come for you to be born, He sanctified you, set you apart, and blessed you in Him. Man did not form you. Man did not set you apart nor sanctify you. Man is not your enemy. Satan, the accuser, is the enemy of God and all those made in God's image. Unfortunately, Satan uses whoever will yield themselves available to him, allowing him to lead them into demonic suppression.

Ephesians 1:4 (NLT) says, *"Even before He made the world, God loved us and chose us in Christ to be holy and without fault in His eyes."* We were known by God and chosen, in spite of our bad decisions, in spite of our bad choices. God has not chosen our difficult paths, but He will use them. It is not God's desire that we make bad decisions, but He is still God in our bad decisions. It is not God's desire that we make bad choices, but He is still God in our bad choices. God is not taken aback of the results of our lives as others may be. He is so wonderful that when we choose to receive His Son Jesus as Lord of our lives, we give Him permission to come in and walk with us along the way, and He will rectify situations, decisions, and circumstances.

God does not reverse time to allow things in our lives to line up; however, it is in the processes of walking out our situations, our boo-boos, and our messes that God walks alongside of us and His grace overshadows us. Remember, Romans 8:28 says, *"And we know that all things work together for good to those who love God, to those who are the called according to His purpose."* God uses our situations, which may be horrendous, to work together for good to those who love God, to those who are the called according to His purpose. However, it is not an overnight process. Sometimes it takes years for us to actually walk in the place of God where we say like David, *"It is good for me that I have been afflicted, That I may learn Your Statutes."* (Psalm 119:71, NKJV). God has a way of redeeming our times. He takes our mistakes, hurts, pains, divorces, criminal acts, abandonments, and even abortions, and He redeems them all.

First Peter 5:10 (NKJV) says, *"But may the God of all grace, who called us to His eternal glory by Christ Jesus, after you have suffered a while, perfect, establish, strengthen, and settle you."* Praise the Lord that after we have suffered a little while, God, the God of all grace, the One who has called us in His Son, Christ Jesus, will Himself restore us. What did you lose? Did you lose your self-worth while the world had a handle on your life? God is here to restore everything you lost. In your situations and circumstances that were overwhelming, were you at a place of uncertainty? Your Heavenly Father is here to confirm to you that He is for you and He is not against you. Do you find that you need strength to keep going or to stay in the game of life? Your heavenly Father is here to equip you with strength and to establish you, to make your imprint here on the earth where you impact the lives of those in your sphere of influence. Your heavenly Father is here to give you a sure foundation, establish you in Him, and solidify you in Him.

Other fears that we may have had or currently are experiencing have been noted below, along with a definition, description, synonyms, and a few Scripture references for guidance and encouragement regarding each fear.

Insecurity[10]: (1) Lack of confidence or assurance; self-doubt; (2) the quality or state of being insecure; instability; (3) something insecure.

> **Romans 8:31** (NLT) – *What shall we say about such wonderful things as these? If God is for us, who can ever be against us?*

> **Ephesians 1:4-5** (NLT) – *Even before he made the world, God loved us and chose us in Christ to be holy and without fault in his eyes. God decided in advance to adopt us into his own family by bringing us to himself through Jesus Christ.*

> **1 John 4:18** – *There is no fear in love; but perfect love casts out fear, because fear involves torment. But he who fears has not been made perfect in love.*

Comparison[11]: (1) The act of comparing; (2) the state of being compared; (3) a likening; illustration or similitude; comparative estimate or statement; (4) the consideration of two things with regard to some characteristic that is common to both, as the likening of a hero to a lion in courage.

Fear often surrounds comparison, especially if viewed from a negative perspective; we don't believe that we are enough and so we allow fear to undermine our purposes and prohibit us from moving forward, even paralyzing us.

> **Philippians 2:3** (NKJV) – *Let nothing be done through selfish ambition or conceit, but in lowliness of mind let each esteem others better than himself.*

---

[10] https://www.dictionary.com/browse/insecurity#
[11] https://www.dictionary.com/browse/comparison

2 Corinthians 10:12 (NKJV) – *For we dare not class ourselves or compare ourselves with those who commend themselves. But they, measuring themselves by themselves, and comparing themselves among themselves, are not wise.*

Galatians 6:3-5 (NKJV) – *For if anyone thinks himself to be something, when he is nothing, he deceives himself. But let each one examine his own work, and then he will have rejoicing in himself alone, and not in another. For each one shall bear his own load.*

<u>**Unbelief**</u>[12]: The state or quality of not believing; incredulity or skepticism, especially in matters of doctrine or religious faith.

Romans 4:20 (NKJV) – *He did not waver at the promise of God through unbelief, but was strengthened in faith giving glory of God,*

Hebrews 3:12 (NKJV) – *Take care brethren that there not be in any one of you an evil, unbelieving heart that falls away from the Living God.*

Hebrews 11:6 (NKJV) – *But without faith it is impossible to please Him, for he who comes to God must believe that He is, and that He is a rewarder of those who diligently seek Him.*

<u>**Afraid to hope again**</u> – Sometimes, life can grip you in such a way that it will squeeze all the hope you have out of you. One begins to be afraid to hope because hope requires energy to hope again; expectancy

---

[12] https://www.dictionary.com/browse/unbelief

is also required to hope again. But the strength of the Lord can arise in your heart once again and enable you to hope in Him. Allow yourself to hope and trust in Him; He won't let you be ashamed.

> **Romans 10:11** (NKJV) – *For the Scripture says, "Whoever believes on Him will not be put to shame."*

> **Psalm 62:1-2, 5-8** (NKJV) – *Truly my soul silently waits for God; from Him comes my salvation. He only is my rock and my salvation. He is my defense; I shall not be greatly moved. My soul, wait silently for God alone, For my expectation is from Him. He only is my rock and my salvation; He is my defense; I shall not be moved. In God is my salvation and my glory; The rock of my strength, And my refuge, is in God. Trust in Him at all times, you people; Pour out your heart before Him; God is a refuge for us. Selah*

> **Psalms 119:116** – *Uphold me according to Your word, that I may live; And do not let me be ashamed of my hope.*

<u>Uncertainty</u>[13]: – The state of being uncertain, doubt, or hesitancy.

> **Proverbs 3:5-6** – *Trust in the LORD with all your heart, And lean not on your own understanding; In all your ways acknowledge Him, And He shall direct your paths.*

> **Hebrews 10:35** – *Therefore do not cast away your confidence, which has a great reward.*

---

[13] https://www.dictionary.com/browse/uncertainty

Psalms 121:3-8 – *He will not allow your foot to be moved; He who keeps you will not slumber. Behold, He who keeps Israel shall neither slumber nor sleep. The LORD is your keeper; the LORD is your shade on your right hand. The sun shall not strike you by day, nor the moon by night. The LORD shall preserve you from all evil; He shall preserve your life.*

Say this with me: "Fear has held me back long enough!" Say it a few more times, then pause and give ample thought to what you have just decreed. Make it more personal by saying, "FEAR, you have held me back long enough!" If you believe that, how will it change the narrative of your life going forward? What will you do differently if FEAR was no longer one of your colleagues? I am not asking you about finances, support, a building, a title, nor a platform; what would you do if FEAR was taken out of the equation? If you knew that God said to you, "I'm propelling you forward," what would you do first? Take a moment and write it down.

Layer Eight ~ Perfect Pride

I did a lot of work and participated in a lot of programs to show that I was a part of all that God was doing both in my church and in my sphere of influence. I was abreast of all that was going on. I involved myself in a lot of outside and ministry-related activities and I participated mainly because the work gave me value. Not so much because my name was called but because within myself I felt needed, significant, and sometimes even useful. The work which I did was all good work, do not get me wrong, but some of the programs and events were not God's good, acceptable and perfect will for that particular season of my life. But God allowed it and therefore used it, however, He did not choose it; I chose it, and due to my people-pleasing tendencies, I got involved in it.

But yet, God is still so very faithful. He used those times in my life and even those situations and circumstances where I was looking and searching for valid approval and the feelings of being significant, even with the work of my hands. God used these situations to peel off layers of insecurity which buried the real me. I have come to realize that our God is an opportunistic God, taking advantage of every opportunity. Just as the Scripture says, *"And we know that all things work together for good to those who love God, to those who are the called according to His purpose."* Romans 8:28 (NKJV). God sees my heart. Friend, God sees your heart. He knows the insecurities that I wrestled with and my continually attempting to find security, validation, affirmation and people-pleasing in outside activities instead of finding them in Him. However, God did not give up on me. He will not give up on you. I did not all of a sudden become a writer.

I was a writer from birth; from the foundations of the world, and I was NOT a prostitute or a drug addict from the foundations of the world. The enemy of my soul used these acts, vices, mechanisms, distractions, distorted and perverted attractions, and methods of deception to prevent, delay, and ultimately stop me. But again, these were not chosen by God and although He did not choose them, He did use them to be a part of the message of deliverance, love, salvation, and hope in my life and for others to whom I have the wonderful opportunity to serve.

Pride can be very tricky, though. When you have challenges or struggle with low self-worth or low self-esteem, over the course of time, you tend to find your value in the things that you do – especially if you become very good at them. **Your work becomes your worth**. The work that you do can become a showcase of your talents by which you gain value, approval, and significance. Instead of seeing yourself as beautiful inwardly and outwardly, gifted and highly skilled for the work for which the Lord has graced your life with for His glory, you begin to see the work, performance, job, ministry, or accomplishments as valid points of "success" in your portfolio. This extremely thin line is crossed when you begin to own such success, value, approval, and significance like you would own your worth, self-esteem, and beauty; it becomes the "outward beauty" that you struggle to have.

How does pride fall in? Pride raises its ugly and desperate head much like a person who knows he or she is beautiful. They begin to cherish their looks in an alarming manner. But again, this is so very subtle that only their make-up artist really knows. In this case, only God knows, until the situation begins to unravel and you begin to reveal who you really are. By this time, people are already seeing you as unapproachable or snooty, and they may be making snide comments about a queen or king mentality you have developed. Now that you have this picture in mind, think of it in terms of the person who gets their worth and value from the functions that they perform. They tend to be performance driven because this is what they are "thirsty" for. It does not begin as wanting a platform, but it is not long until their hunger develops into a platform to be seen as being the best or doing the best. This is where and how pride enters. Pride does not enter in as a showy coin; no, pride enters in like a small breeze that keeps turning, turning, and turning until a full wind has developed, blowing everything out of its way. It takes time before pride rises up, though, due to its subtle nature. Again, it begins with a small breeze.

    I label this tendency in my life as perfect pride. For me, perfect pride shows up as the work on the job that I did and the feelings I had that the work had to be perfect. There is nothing wrong with desiring to do a good and perfect job. In fact, one should have a great work ethic, inclusive of doing a good job. I have worked in both the legal and medical fields for more than 37 years. I tend to gravitate to the legal field more due to the financial benefits and rewards. I began my work in the legal field under the camouflage title of "combat" secretary. This type of secretary was known to have a high tolerance for emotional pain, endurance, and tough skin. I missed out on the tough skin part, but because I had an excellent work ethic, high tolerance for emotional pain, patience, and endurance, I was the best one running for the combat title. The combat pay, which is what the HR administrators used to call it, was that a secretary was rewarded financially for working and remaining with difficult attorneys, especially the ones no one would or could work with. Most of the time, these were older or middle-aged attorneys who were above the status of exceptional lawyers. Their tempers, attitudes, and the like were often cause for secretaries leaving for lunch and not returning.

    Here is where I would often come in. I needed the money, being a single mom. I could not afford to quit the job or tell them to take "this job and shove it." I probably did not have to, but I felt like I had to endure, and that is just what I did. I stayed on the job until the attorney saw that I was not leaving. Over time, often years, he/she would get used to me, I would get used to him or her, and we continued to work together. Because of the attorney's difficult demeanor, being a challenge to work with, and with my low self-esteem, I always took their remarks about my work personally, like they were critiquing me as a person. They were not; they were simply trying to get a work product completed and because I did not know the difference at the time, I did not know how to differentiate what I did from who I was. I took everything in and made it a part of me; therefore, it was all personal. The only way that I could get through it was to do an excellent or perfect job and produce a perfect work product.

But no one can do a job perfectly every single time. I had to learn that. I had to learn that my job or my work product was not me, although my personality, my ethics, and my ability to perform the job and see the project through was a reflection of me as an employee. The professional critiquing of the job was not an attack on my person. I had to learn that, and this is still a challenge for me on occasions, although it is no longer a deep area of struggle.

The difference is that the Lord is working with me on valuing myself, my time, my skills, and my knowledge. If there is a mistake, a mishap, or professional criticism, it is the job, the product, the assignment, or my understanding or lack thereof of the assignment or the product, but it is NOT me as a person. Therefore, if the assignment does not go well or if the job or work product has significant mistakes and needs to be thoroughly redone, I am not to walk away with my head down and curse myself with words like, "I performed like an idiot; I'm just stupid" or "I should have done a better job at this; I really must be dumb." No; I truly no longer attack myself in that manner. When I would get back negative reports of my work product, it used to be a bucket of ice cream and a whole chocolate cheesecake for sure; now, my response is back to the drawing board and how can I improve.

This can be a significant challenge for people who are not able to differentiate from the work product, performance, accomplishments, functions, a job assignment, or ministry work as, separate from one's personhood, especially for those who struggle with low self-esteem. Because I would often feel attacked, both at work and in ministry, due to my low self-esteem, I would internalize the remarks negatively, even if the remarks were as positive as they could possibly be. Can you imagine the enemy's deception working in the mind of the individual with low self-esteem every time they received instructions to change, add, renew, delete, update, etc.? The person with low self-esteem is taking all this personally. The enemy is distorting their view of what was said and even what the person meant. Literally, everything is amplified negatively. I am highlighting this because I have had this play out for me on several different platforms, and it was not a good feeling nor a good battle; truthfully, it was often a battle that I lost because I was dealing with it personally instead of professionally.

The ultimate deception of the enemy is perfect pride. He knew exactly where he was trying to lead me, and I was almost there, headed for the place of perfect pride. Perfect pride is where you no longer work to simply produce a work product, perform an assignment, do the work of ministry, or function within a work or ministry assignment; you do so under the auspices that everything has to be absolutely perfect. You work night and day to have it be seen as perfect because it is a reflection of **you**. The focus has shifted from the Lord God Jesus Christ to **you**. From this perspective, when it is perceived as an assignment done in excellence, a smile comes across your face, your chest rises, your heart is elevated, and pride is lifted up a few inches higher. This continues, assignment after assignment, until it is all about **you**. It is no longer about the job; your attitude becomes, "No one can do this but me," "I know how my attorneys like his/her work product," or "I know how the doctor I work for like things done and he/she likes them done a certain way; only I can do it like they want it." Have you ever heard or said that before? I used to be one of the persons saying those phrases.

This is the deception the enemy of our soul uses, and I took it in, believing the sound of it because it fed my ego that someone needed me and I was valued; I was worth something to someone. Pride developed for all the wrong reasons (though there is no right reason for pride to develop in one's life), but the invisible goal that I was working towards was my self-worth and my self-esteem, fed by the pride that I was receiving from accolades I received for a good job, a great performance, a wonderful accomplishment and/or function, or a work or ministry related assignment completed. On days that I felt good, I was having an up day and my work (my worth/esteem) was on point. However, on days when the sun refused to shine, the mistakes I made had me feeling like I was playing handball with the sidewalk, and I continued to work night and day until things were back to perfect and I received the great compliments. That is perfect pride.

Never let your self-esteem cause you to not always surrender the glory of everything that you accomplish to God! We are to be thankful for all our accomplishments, every opportunity, every opened door, the works of our hands, and assignments, jobs, or tasks we perform. We are always to take a healthy sense of pride in our work, in every area, even if it is cleaning toilets or mopping floors. Be thankful for it, do it with excellence, and thank God for it, but never allow the compliments to frame you or dictate to your self-worth or self-esteem.

A priceless gift received only from spending time with the Holy Spirit and lingering in His presence is the revelation that external activity (job performance, ministry accomplishments, and all that this may entail) will never bring one to a place of internal significance. Our internal significance (self-worth, self-esteem) is developed in the presence of the Lord. The Lord's presence, along with healthy family communication and interactions, healthy friendships, healthy love relationships, continued learning, and educational development and growth develops within His children a healthy and courageous mindset (heart) of self-esteem. This takes time, years even, and may not be a complete or finished work just because one is doing well or feeling better about oneself, especially when there has been a significant amount of emotional trauma; healing and relearning needs to take place. Part of relearning is unlearning old habits, old methods of deception, old ways of thinking and processing of both internal and external communications, and old systems of understanding and receiving information into your heart and mind. Once your heart and mind have been renewed by the Word of God, spiritual growth is the result. Your internal development and your continued growth move you forward to give right placement in your heart to the Lord, His work, your work, and your perception of the work that you do.

Noted below are a few healing scriptures that I use to pray and meditate through this idea of perfect pride.

2 Corinthians 10:17-18 (NKJV) – *But "he who glories, let him glory in the LORD." For not he who commends himself is approved, but whom the Lord commends.*

2 Corinthians 10:18 (NLT) – *When people commend themselves, it doesn't count for much. The important thing is for the Lord to commend them.*

1 John 2:15-17 (NKJV) – *Do not love the world or the things in the world. If anyone loves the world, the love of the Father is not in him. For all that is in the world – the lust of the flesh, the lust of the eyes, and the pride of life – is not of the Father but is of the world. And the world is passing away, and the lust of it; but he who does the will of God abides forever.*

Ultimately, I had to learn to not focus on self-worth nor self-esteem. The subtle scheme of the enemy is to keep one focused on oneself; if you're always looking to yourself or looking at yourself, the desires of the flesh, what you have, what you do not have, or what you think you need, these thoughts will eventually overtake you. You will get caught up in the desires of the eyes and taking pride in the things you have, the accomplishments completed and the accolades received. This is adapting ourselves and our desires to that of the culture.

Beloved, be free! Immerse yourself in the presence of the Lord and in the writings of His Word. Allow His Word to be the permeating element in your life and heart. Too many things in this culture are vying for your most important part: your attention and your worship. If your attention is being focused on you and yourself alone, you have no time nor ability to think of others and the need that others may have for the beauty, help and ministry that only you can bring them. Again, be free. Seek Christ and not compliments, approvals, or endorsements for your accomplishments. Seek the Lord and listen for His approval of you. The Lord's approval is so much more refreshing and life-changing, and it promises true rewards, both here and eternally.

How I Moved from There

Layer Nine ~ Free Indeed

He Whom the Son Sets Free is Free Indeed

Although there was not a voice for Christ in my home until later in life when my mom accepted Christ in her senior years, God's presence was welcomed in my life. God connected me with a neighborhood friend whose family led me to Christ and began taking me to church. I remember this well; I was in the seventh grade. It was through this family and in this Pentecostal church where I met God for the first time. I was saved in a small storefront church that was filled with the presence of the Holy Spirit, and I received Christ as my savior.

While this was my first introduction to Jesus Christ where I accepted Him as my Savior, the wonderful Holy Spirit made alive that which seemed to be dying on the vine. I was brought back to life, and instead of simply existing, I began to have hope even among the turmoil that I was experiencing in my home. Glory to God! Hope was birthed within me, and I felt the power of God rescuing me from the plan of the enemy. To be truthful, I did not know about the enemy's plan, but God knew about it from the beginning of time and God's plans trumped the enemy's. God confessed over my life, "I did not choose it but I will use it. Watch as I use this catastrophe of molestation for My glory!" God declared that He would take every fiber of my being and make me into the daughter that He called me to be.

During those quiet and dark times of my life as a young girl, I developed a love for reading. God developed in me a love for the

Word of God. He gave me a hunger and a thirst for His Word. I did not even recognize it as such, but I was so hungry for God! I was so hungry for what I now recognize as love, peace, and normalcy. God brought this into my life. I was able to see that in the Old Testament: the challenges, the difficulties, and the distraught home life that Hagar had; the disruption of Naomi and Ruth; and the challenge and mishandling of Tamar. I saw how God brought them out into their own wealthy places. When everyone wrote them off and dismissed them in their difficulty, God stood for them, gave them a name in their story, and allowed those who would read their story to see His hands bringing deliverance to their lives. I read the Gospels in the New Testament and fell in love with the differences and personalities of each gospel narrator. God not only used His Word but also songs, both hymns and gospel music, during that time to pour in the oil and the wine over my spirit and bring healing to my mind, to my emotions, and to my spirit.

God allowed healing to take place that is still being manifested in my life currently. God will perform His Word, and His Word will work. The Word will work until the work is done. Hallelujah! We are so used to when things do not work, we move on to the next thing and we discount the work that has gone before, but not God. Not the Holy Spirit. God works until the work is complete. Did He not work from Genesis until Malachi? Did He not work from Matthew until Revelation? God works until the work is complete, even if that work may take years, generations, and even lifetimes. Our job, our duty, and our endeavor is to stay in the game and allow God to do the work until it is finished. Philippians 1:6 (NKJV) says: *"Being confident of this very thing, that He who has begun a good work in you will complete it until the Day of Jesus Christ."* God will finish what He started. He is the author and the finisher of our faith (Hebrews 12:2). God will finish it.

I was not aware of the demonic forces that were against me, evidently from birth, but I am very aware of the enemy's strategy now. This is the enemy's chief strategy. From this root, spawns all of his trails of destruction: John 10:10 (NKJV) says, *"The thief does not come except to steal, and to kill, and to destroy. I have come that they might have life, and that they may have it more abundantly."* Now let's unpack this scripture as it pertains to the situation at hand. Who is the thief? **The thief** is the enemy of our souls. He is a thief and God through the Bible labels and calls him a thief. The thief comes **to steal**; he is one who steals especially stealthily, secretly, or without open force, one guilty of theft or larceny. The thief comes **to kill**; he will slay or slaughter for any purpose, and by extension to immolate – to kill or offer as a sacrifice, especially by burning, like the phrase "my dreams went up in smoke." The thief comes **to destroy**; this means to put out of the way entirely, abolish, to put an end to, ruin, render useless, to declare that one must be put to death, to devote or give over to eternal misery in hell, to perish, or to be lost, ruined, to lose. Now do you see the plan of the enemy for your life? I see the plan of the enemy for my life, and it is crystal clear to me. Do you see why he has attacked you from the time your mom discovered she was pregnant with you? It was the enemy's strategy as a thief in your life: to steal, to kill and to destroy.

But why was the devil after me like that? I am not a person of significance, at least that is what I thought. Perhaps you have thought to yourself that same idea. But, you and I are made in the image of our Heavenly Father. Because we are made in the image of our God, the enemy will fight us tooth and nail until we close our eyes on this side of heaven and open our eyes in the Kingdom of God. The enemy does not know your destiny, nor can he see into the future. But this is key: the enemy is consistent. The enemy is on his job fervently, and the only paycheck he will ever receive is burning in hell.

But here is the catch: the enemy desires to take as many people to hell with him as he can. He does not know your future; the enemy is not a prophet. At the beginning of time, he was cast down from Heaven and took a one third of Heaven's angelic host with him because he rose up in pride and set himself to rebel against Almighty God. "For you have said in your heart: *'I will ascend into heaven, I will exalt my throne above the stars of God; I will also sit on the mount of the congregation on the farthest sides of the north; I will ascend above the heights of the clouds, I will be like the Most High.'"* (Isaiah 14:13-14, NKJV). God said, *"Yet, you shalt be brought down to Sheol, to the lowest depths of the pit"* (Isaiah 14:15, NKJV).

Once pride and rebellion were found in Satan, he had to go. The stronghold that the enemy tries to build in our lives is that he continues to work on our minds by sending thoughts of hatred, reminding us of our sins, attempting to use guilt and shame from previous life choices, attempting to bring about curses, and provoking thoughts of rebellion and temptations. He has worked on humanity for centuries, and he has seen people fall, falter, give into temptation, lie, cheat, steal, and come up short. Yet if they turn to Almighty God, confess their sins, and receive Jesus Christ as Lord, Satan knows that the war is over and he has lost. However, if he can fight you and convince you to give up in your war, to stop praying, that your fasting does not work and it never will work, that you cannot retain the Word of God, that the Word of God is not relevant for this day and time, or that you cannot memorize the Word of God let alone pray the Word of God, then he knows that he got you and he knows that he has built a formidable stronghold in your mind. The devil is consistent. He never gives up; we give up. We stop. We cease. But the enemy never gives up. This is how he has deceived so many souls for the lake of fire and brimstone because he never gives up.

The enemy comes into our lives during infancy and as children who cannot fight on our own. The enemy attempts to steal, especially stealthily, secretly, or without open force. Most times, especially as his battle is in the mind, he attempts to steal right from under us by planting seeds of abuse that develop into low self-esteem, seeds of anger, seeds of depression, or seeds of uncertainty, especially in our childhood, right under the watchful (or unwatchful) eyes of those in authority. The enemy attempts to kill, to slay, or to slaughter for **any** purpose. I believe the enemy does this so perfectly by planting seeds of generational curses of alcohol, drug addiction, perversion, depression, and other mind diseases that are not readily and easily diagnosable. The enemy wants us to give up on ourselves so that his work is relatively easy; no need to kill you if you kill yourself.

I submit to you that the disruptions the enemy has brought to your life have been his attempts to steal, kill, and destroy your life. Unfortunately, these disruptions did not stop in our infancy; that was only the beginning. They were designed to abort God's purpose beforehand. The enemy knows that if he can be consistent in our lives by continuing to send torment, disruption, and delay in the forms of child abuse, molestation, rape, drug addiction, alcohol addiction, shame, prostitution, guilt, low self-esteem, depression, rejection, hatred for one's self, rebellion and perversion, jail, prison, husbands that beat us, boyfriends that misuse us, and even parents that do not take care of us as they should, this will work toward destroying us. But as we accept Christ as Lord and Savior, we WIN! The book of Revelation says that we win as the bride of Christ! As an individual believer, Christ desires that we win at life NOW. Glory to God! That's my desire for myself and for you that we win at life. The believer in Christ WINS.

Refuse to live beneath your privilege and potential. John 8:36 (NKJV) says, *"Therefore, if the Son makes you free, you shall be free indeed."* The revelation of this scripture is captured in its context of John 8:31-35. Jesus was sharing with the Jews who believed Him, *"If you abide in My word you are my disciples indeed"* (verse 31). The underlying thought is that because one believes in Christ, one will abide in His Word and is therefore His disciple; therefore, the truth that one *knows* shall make one free. The word "know" is the Greek word *ginosko*, and it means to perceive, understand, recognize, gain knowledge, realize, or come to know. In other words, there is a progression of knowledge which can be attained, therefore it is my experience that as one comes into a personal relationship with Christ by accepting Christ as Lord and Savior, believing in His Word, and experiencing His Word, that person is made free.

What are we made free from? We are made free from the slavery and bondage of the enemy. The more we attain the Word of Christ and make it personal and applicable in our lives by walking in it, believing it, and adhering to it, the truth of the Word is revealed and bondages are broken. The more truth we read, receive, and adhere to, the more bondages and negative thought patterns are broken in our lives. We are set free by the truth. We are made free by the truth – the truth that we know, the truth that we believe and adhere to.

What bondage do you have in your life? What place remains a stronghold in your life? Have you sought the Word of the Lord in this area? I guarantee you that as you seek Christ in these places of slavery, of your mind, your appetites, your will, and your emotions, the Word of God can set you free. Jesus died to make you and I free! But we must choose to believe Him. We must choose to read and receive His Word, apply it to our lives and walk in it. When we do sin, we need to repent and seek Christ's forgiveness, and then these entanglements and distractions that came to get us off track will melt off of us like wax.

I did not have to ask for deliverance from some things in my life because the Word found them in my life, attacked them, and obliterated them. It was the Word of God that came in, worked on my heart, worked on my mind, changed my spirit, and lifted a beautifully buried flower from underneath years of dirt and manure. Through the Word of God, the dirt was cleansed, and the manure was used to strengthen my life through the situations that came against me. God used the manure of the situations and circumstances that were causing me to remain a slave. He used it all to build me up. Through His Word, He called me into freedom as a child of God, an heir of salvation, no longer an orphan and even more so, ***no longer a slave***. Slaves do not have access as a son or daughter does. A slave is not a part of the family, nor does a slave have a part of the family's inheritance, but as a child of God, we are an heir of salvation.

You may have been buried by dirt and manure in your life. You do not feel like a child of God, but you feel like a slave – ashamed of what you have done and buried under the manure of decisions, choices, or circumstances of your life. You may feel buried beneath the weight of what you have gone through. Perhaps it was a marriage gone awry, and you are carrying the weight upon your shoulders. Maybe it is the decision of the courts that due to the life you are living, your children have been stripped away from you. Perhaps you are caught up in a lifestyle that you are inwardly fed up with, but you will not admit it to yourself or your friends, and you continue to live this life knowing that it is stealing from you. Maybe you are tired, but you are continuing to tell yourself that this is the life that you have chosen and you do not deserve anything better. Maybe this book has found you in a prison cell due to mistakes and bad choices that others who said they were your friends did to you because they proved to be enemies instead. You are now paying a hefty price and you are missing your kids and family.

Friend, God says to you, *"Stand fast therefore in the liberty by which Christ has made us free, and do not be entangled again with a yoke of bondage."* (Galatians 5:1, NKJV). Christ set us free so that we could live our lives for his glory in freedom; not going back and being entangled again in the yoke of bondage which brought about slavery. It was for freedom that Christ has set us free. Receive Christ, receive His truth, receive His Word, and finally be made free. Let freedom begin in your heart. Once freedom rules in your heart, it is only a matter of time until your mind will be set free from the enslavements and bondages of our enemy, Satan. You have a right to be free whereby you are free inside and out, spiritually and emotionally. Be free, friend – Christ has come to set us free.

After many, many years of internal struggle, I am free. Obtaining my freedom in Christ was simply receiving Christ into my life. However, this truth and this freedom have not been obtained easily. I had to choose to receive God's Word and apply it in and to my life, moment by moment. This is not easy, however, it is a loving act of obedience. Obedience does not always feel good, but as you grow in love with Christ, your obedience becomes an act of love, an act of your willingness to obey out of love. Choosing obedience may look like remaining silent when you desire to say something mean, nasty, and hurtful about or to someone. It is a choice to be obedient in every area of your life. It is called choosing Holiness – the Lord's way of releasing your will and receiving Christ's will for your life. Our lives are not our own. Our lives and our salvation were purchased by Christ. The Apostle Paul, in his first letter to the Corinthian church, spoke to them about glorifying God in both their physical body and in their spirit: *"Or do you know that your body is the temple of the Holy Spirit who is in you, whom you have from God and you are not your own? For you were bought at a price; therefore glorify God in your body and in your spirit which are God's"* (1 Corinthians 6:19-20, NKJV).

Friend, I say to you just as the Apostle Paul said, you are not your own. As you are reading this book, Christ has been calling you into a life of redemption and a life of love. Say yes to Christ. Hear Him calling and gently whispering to you of His love for you. He has brought you out of some dire situations. Recognize that He has spared your life that time and now this time. Surrender your heart to Him. Ask Him to come into your heart and your life and simply abide with you as you abide with Him. Begin to read the book of John in a Bible translation that breaks the Word down for you so that after you read it you can remember it; your heart can take hold of the Word and make it easy to ***apply*** the Word to your life, moment by moment.

If you are currently not a believer and you would like to accept Christ as your Savior, or if you have backslidden from principles and precepts of your previous life in Christ, please read the prayer below and make it your own.

Prayer

God, I'm a sinner and I believe You sent Your Son, Jesus Christ, to die on the cross for my sins.
I believe Jesus Christ suffered a horrendous death and on the third day, He rose from the dead.
Lord Jesus, I invite you into my heart to be my Lord and Savior.
I receive You, Lord Jesus.
Thank you for giving Your life for me.
Renew my mind through Your Word and help me serve You daily.
In Jesus' name I pray, Amen.

_____

Name and Date

As a new believer in Christ, make it a priority to pray and read your Bible daily. If you eat breakfast, lunch, and dinner daily, read your Bible daily. Prayer is talking to God and allowing Him to talk to you through His Word. God speaks in several ways, but one of the main ways is through His Word in the Bible. Another way God speaks is through the Holy Spirit. He may speak to you or simply be an impression upon your heart. Reading the Word of God allows you to learn of Him; it is a mirror whereby we as Christians can look into the love letters of our Heavenly Father and experience His will for our lives. Pray and ask God to lead you to a Bible-believing church that you can attend. Once found, join and attend the church as often as you can; this will help you with connecting with other Christian believers which will be a help to you in terms of fellowship and accountability.

Remember, there is a body of believers praying for you as you read His Word and as you journey on to know the Lord.

Trust My Silence

Trust God's Silence

Psalm 28:1 (NKJV)
To You I will cry, O LORD my Rock:
Do not be silent to me, lest if You are silent to me,
I become like those who go down to the pit.

This is a hard story to tell, like most that I've written thus far. However, I must share it as it has learning principles for someone who may read the book, and I pray that their life will be impacted in Christ and for Christ.

I am a single woman and have been single and celibate for 26 years now. Only by the power and grace of God has the Lord kept me from dangers seen and unseen and from people who would have mistaken my kindness for weakness and taken advantage of me. This story is written to highlight God's faithfulness even in my ignorance, all the while my heart remains obedient to serve the Lord wholeheartedly.

Not long ago, during a distressed time in my life, my mother had passed away and my oldest brother had died three months later. My emotions were not settled to say the least, and yet God was with me all the way, comforting me and giving me peace. People were coming and going, as they do during times of loss in one's family; however, an acquaintance alerted a friend of theirs to the loss I was experiencing in my family and this gentleman friend of theirs was unexpectedly at our family service making an appearance in my life. Something did not seem right, but my emotions were not settled. However, I remained quiet and simply desired to watch and see the outcome. Well, some things unfolded, and I allowed my feelings to get ahead of me. Before long, I began to see only what I had imagined in my own mind, creating a space that was never meant to be occupied. Women often speculate and create situations which are not really evolving like we think, except in the places of our own mind. Unfortunately, soon after because of the situation we created in our mind, we end up with and in a situation, even if only in our own mind. This happened with me, but thank God it remained **only in my own mind**.

Thank God, the Holy Spirit did not allow anything else to be so! What my emotions caused me to smile and grin about was simply what I played off in my own mind and was never meant to be by the good, acceptable, and perfect will of God. The Holy Spirit kept me and did not let me go off the deep end! Nothing happened except within the confines of my own mind. The enemy desired to use that and get me all tangled up, but God wouldn't allow it to be so. As it turned out, life as I knew it continued to move ahead and what I thought was coming or developing never even began.

During this time, I was able to take a short vacation and simply get alone with God for a week of intense prayer and fasting. I cried, moaned, meditated, worshiped, and delved into the Word of God because I did not understand what was going on. I was questioning God. Did I miss something? Did I do something? What in the world took place that I am not even aware of? The most awakening part of this was that during this entire time, the Holy Spirit appeared silent to me. Even though my heart, conscience, and mind were clear and at peace, the process of how things started, developed (or did not develop), and then ended without a finish or one that I saw coming, blew me away. Yet I was at peace.

However, I had to know. God, what was this for? What was the lesson you wanted me to walk away with from this situation? What were you teaching me? I did not want to miss this, and I definitely did not want to repeat it. What is the **IT**, Lord? I kept asking the Holy Spirit, what is the **IT** in this lesson that you want me to learn?

Finally, on day 6 of my short vacation, a gentle yet deep impression in my spirit rose up like a beautiful fragrance" *"Trust My Silence."* Right then, I simply wept. I wept before the Lord because right then I knew that He had seen all that had (not) taken place, and **IT** was yet what He had allowed. This time of testing was allowed to see what I would do. That was the **IT**. Would I run off and "make things happen," or would I simply wait until all obedience and righteousness had been fulfilled? Was I to go on human information and move by my own understanding? Or was I to trust the Lord with ALL my heart and lean not to my own understanding?

I was to acknowledge God in ALL of my ways so that He could direct my paths and not accept something simply because it was *available.* Many times before, I had missed it and messed up my life because I accepted something simply because it was or appeared to be *available*, but it was not God's good, acceptable, and perfect will for my life. This was my test; it was my **IT**, and when I heard the Holy Spirit say, *"Trust My Silence,"* that was all that needed to be said.

"Trust My Silence" was the Holy Spirit's way of telling me to *wait*. Don't take another step until you've heard from God first. Don't move until you hear from God about the next thing to say, do, don't say, or don't do. **WAIT**! That's what "Trust My Silence" means. Trust the Lord's silence when everyone is chattering in your ear giving their opinion, their commentary, and their description of what they believe is best for your life. The Holy Spirit knows the end from the beginning, and He knows the PLANS that He has written out for your life. Stop moving and flowing according to someone else's desires for your life. They are not going to be there when things go awry to pick up the pieces of your broken and shattered life when you step out of the perfect will of God. The Holy Spirit will be there, and if you allow

Him to, He will lead, guide, and direct your every move, including your stops and your starts. It may be painful, but ***don't move***. Don't go and push through unless the Holy Spirit is telling you to do so. If the Holy Spirit is silent and He's telling you to trust His silence, remain still. Women are enthusiastic, creative, energetic, entrepreneurial, ambitious, and we make things happen. Men are the lion, the hunter, the producer, the achiever, and they especially push to make something happen. However, I implore you to be led by God. Allow Him to finish what He began in your life. Don't rush to finish your own story and put a false period at what appears to be an end. Wait, trust, believe, and watch God unfold your story as a beautiful flower or a beautiful prized automobile that was in the junk yard. Be remade from the *inside out* into a prized possession, not to just sit in a showroom, but to be showcased for God's glory.

Remember, friends, when you're faced with a situation and the direction that you desire to take is not clearly known and approved by the Holy Spirit, seek His guidance no matter how long it takes. Wait for it, and don't move until He speaks. Stay at His feet. Stay in His Word. Linger in His presence until His good, acceptable, and perfect will is made clear. That may simply be a "Trust My Silence" moment. If it is, simply wait and don't move. It's in the brilliance of His silence that His good, acceptable, and perfect will is revealed.

Lastly Spoken

A Prostitute No Longer ~ A Word for the Body of Christ

You no longer have to play small. You play small because that is how you see yourself. That may be how you feel, but I say walk by faith and not by sight. Walk by faith, not by how you feel. You are on your way. The enemy knows that the battle has now turned, strength has risen, and increased angelic activity is noticeable. You, the Church, are praying; you are fighting through fasting and My Word is strengthening you. The enemy is aware, but his awareness is too late. You have been awakened to the victorious destiny I have accomplished for you. You are not the victim; you are the victor.

My heart's cry is for the Church, the body of Christ, His bride. We the people of God are the Bride of Christ. A man does not give His bride over to another. Christ gave Himself for His bride, and He will not see His bride hold to herself that which is not her husband. Let us remember that the Lord is a jealous God. His name is Jealous – Jehovah Qanah, which means Jealous God. The bride of Christ is worth being jealous over. After all, her salvation and her destiny were purchased with the blood of the Son of God, Jesus, the Lamb of God, slain from the foundation of the world.

But keep in mind that our Lord is not jealous as humans are jealous. No, our Lord's jealousy and zeal for His bride is with great compassion, unquenchable fire, and love to protect the bride from outside forces that are aimed to harm and hurt her. Unfortunately, she sometimes does not realize it, and thus she takes idols into her bosom, even for a short period of time. Beloved bride, our Heavenly Father would not have it be so. Idols only prevent you from fully, truthfully, and whole-heartedly loving our Savior. Idols will not share heart space, neither will our Lord and Savior. Idols wound, demolish, and kill (kill, steal, and destroy), but our Lord and Savior has brought to us light. Jesus is the light of the world, and we belong to Him.

No longer chase after lovers promising you platforms, wealth, riches, and notoriety. These idols simply want nothing more but your heart, your night of passion, and then to absorb you among the other trophies of their conquest. Be not like those around you; be not like those of this culture. For I say to you, the fashion, the culture, and this world are soon fading away. Come into my presence as a bride comes into the presence of her bridegroom, fully aware of who I am and all that I desire to give you and place before your feet. You belong to Me, and I belong to you. Let not another in.

Acknowledgements

To all my family and friends who encouraged me to write this book for more than 30 years, thank YOU! I hesitated, procrastinated, and even denied that it truly was my assignment to do so, but it would never leave me. It simply would never leave me. I'm so glad I was never able to put it down. I carried it in my spirit until God gave me the strength and the courage to give birth to His dream for me and my passion.

To Pastor Joseph Simpkins and your beloved wife, Juanita Simpkins – thank you for rescuing me and my children from the shelter. To Mother Verdell Simpkins who is now in Heaven – Mother Verdell, as you've joined the great cloud of witnesses which the book of Hebrews speaks of, I simply say thank you, as I've done so many times before while you were still with us. Thank you for your love for the saints and the work of ministry. Only Heaven will tell of the many lives and souls that were saved because of your oneness in Kingdom ministry with your husband. Take your rest, Mother Verdell, we'll see you soon. Sister Juanita Simpkins, thank you for being a woman of God who served the Lord in sacrificial singleness and holiness until the day of God's choosing and release for a wonderful life of ministry alongside your husband. You are a beautiful witness of the life and love of a sold-out woman of God!

Thank you, former Pastors Jimmy and Rev. Mary Louise Campbell! Your labor, love, faithfulness, and wisdom throughout the years have always provided a foundation for the many souls who have come through the open doors of Harvest Temple Church of God (HTCOG). Like most of those who have gone on to pastor churches under your tutelage, you have urged us to be faithful. I know no other faithful man and woman in the Gospel like you. Thank you for your great work and leadership in the ministry.

Thank you, Dr. Kenneth and Evangelist Rev. Janice Hill for your wisdom and guidance during your tenure at HTCOG. Your love and genuine care for the saints will never go unnoticed. Your ministry and teachings solidified within me the discipline of serving with the heart of a pastor. When I could not see my way clearly in so many areas, you were always there and continue to be, even now, shining the light of truth and guiding me and others in our walk with Christ.

Pastor Emeritus Rev. Geri and James Izzard, Sr., Rev. Mazie Gause-Carter, Dr. Beverly and Min. Reggie Sargent, Elder David and Sis. Vicki Salley, and last but certainly not least, Rev. Barbara Crowe-White: thank you ALL for your continued love and support.

To Bishop James R. and Rev. Tiffaney Izzard, thank you for remaining a continued anchor in my life. You and Lady Tiffaney remain a profound mentor, coach, and leader not only in my life but also the lives of so many others that you mentor and coach near and far. Your presence is missed greatly, and yet I look forward to the opportunity and privilege to serve once again under your leadership and alongside of you in ministry. *I cherish your friendship.*

Life Builders Church of God Pastors Bishop Rick and Rev. Patricia Felton – your life, your witness of the Holy Spirit, and your continued love and perseverance came along and embraced and sheltered me from the "coming storm." I will forever praise God for your love for me and the saints at Life Builders COG. Life Builders COG Family, there is a prayer which the "old deacons" used to pray: *"Lord, hold him/her up on every leaning side."* You are the post that God **continues to use** to hold me and my family up, *on every leaning side*. Thank YOU!

Elder-Elect StacyPatrice Penn aka *Noble One*, my sister from the same mother and my heart's friend – thank you for your continued support, prayers, and guidance. You continue to believe in me, every step of the way. Thank you! Dcn. Patricia Natalie Williams – over the past 30 years, you've remained a friend. Thank you! Lady Michele Phillips – together _**we are**_ the "Wonder Twins." Thank you for every project where you served alongside of me, for being in the crucible of ministry with me, and never leaving me when things got tough. Thank you for your enduring friendship!

To Elder Ronna Matthews, the greatest worship leader to ever come out of Baltimore, Maryland (in my humble opinion) – I learned worship through the Holy Spirit via YOU. Thank you for every cassette tape, every CD, and a life of sacrificial worship and holy living walked out before God and witnessed by His people. To this day, I still hear worship songs in my spirit that many have forgotten. In the darkest of night, your voice pierces through the thickness of clouds with a song that enraptures me in the Holy Spirit's presence. Thank you for a life of discipline according to Malachi 3:1: _"'Behold, I send My messenger, and he will prepare the way before Me. And the Lord, whom you seek, will suddenly come to His temple, even the Messenger of the covenant, in whom you delight. Behold, He is coming,' says the LORD of hosts."_

To Minister Philip Watson (_Jesus Lover_), thank you for over three years of sound deliverance teaching, prayer, accountability, nurturing and meditation (_Soak Scopes_), conference calls, and Zoom calls with the Deliverance Group. Truly, you have been a moving force in my life. Without the Deliverance Ministry and you adhering to the voice of the Lord to minister to those called alongside of you for such a time as this, this book truly would have continued to be delayed. Thank you, friend.

Prophetess Queen Esther Phillips – without your love, support, prayers, and life coaching, I could have never given birth to Layer Two, "Father to the Fatherless," Psalm 68:5a. You encouraged the baby in my womb to leap and come to life; your love came along and revived and refreshed me. Thank you!!

Lady Lola Oshinowa, thank you for your generous heart towards me in prayers and supplications for me and my family during critical times. I will always hold dear in my heart the nights we spent together in prayer crying out to God for our families and the family of God. Truly you have been a leader in my life and a dear friend. Lucille Freeman and Linda Simpson, you both are the best accountability partners I have experienced on this writing journey. You, Lucille, Linda, and Lady Lola were all cut from the same writing cloth! Thank you, Lucille, for keeping me accountable and always asking me what's next again and again. You kept me on my hands, on my toes, and on my knees! Thank you, Linda, for your kind and gentle prayers and Scriptures for writing (I have learned to be the Lord's priestly pen). Thank you so very much for being there with me and for me. Thank you to my writing coaches, Shelley and CJ Hitz, founders of Christian Book Academy. Thank you for your guidance in writing. All the writing retreats formulated within me a writing discipline. Thank you for connecting Lady Lola, Linda Simpson, Lucille Freeman, and me together. Thank you so very much CJ for when I spoke of quitting the journey, you called me personally, prayed, and encouraged me; through Scripture, you moved me back into position and reminded me of the reason for this book and its devotional. Thank you!

Momma! You're now home with Jesus. For everything I put you through during my tween, teenage, young adult, and adult years, the words "I'm sorry" will never be enough. But, as we stood at your bedside as you were taking your last breath, singing you into the Kingdom, in my heart I knew you'd forgiven me. Momma, I miss you so. I miss the touch of your skin as I would run my hands over your arms when I would visit you in the nursing home. I miss your eyes. When I wanted to talk but there was no one who I could go to, especially in those times when I knew I was wrong, you were always "Jesus with skin on" to me. Your eyes would always say, "It's ok; we'll get through this together." Sometimes you would even look at me with eyes that said, "A hard head makes a soft behind; don't it?" Momma, where did my life go without you in it? The saying is true: there is nothing like a mother's love.

To my daddy. To say the word "daddy" is strange and even foreign to me still. I never knew you in this life. Yet in your own way, you loved Momma and provided for her kids, before I was even born – children that were not your own. Yet because you were the only daddy they knew, you became a father to them. This was your way of showing love to Momma. You provided for me, even briefly, with the money you saved and willed to me in your death. Thank you, Daddy! This was all I knew about you, and yet it was enough to paint a picture of your loving face to me. Your love for me became evident in the story that I would learn about your death. You could not keep quiet about me to save your life; you had to tell of me, even upon the threat of death. A selfish part of me wishes you would have remained silent. Maybe then, I would have seen your face and heard the sound of your voice. *"But love, true love, seeks not its own; nor does it demand its own way"* (1 Corinthians 13:10, paraphrased). Were you loud like I am? Was your laugh robust and jovial like mine? Did your smile light up a dark room like mine? I'll never know, but a girl can definitely wish and even dream.

I never knew you, but I love you, Daddy. I hope you've made Heaven your eternal home so that when I take my final rest, I can awaken to see you.

References

Layer Two – Fatherlessness

1. Alio, A. P., Lewis, C. A., Scarborough, K., Harris, K., & Fiscella, K. (2013). A community perspective on the role of fathers during pregnancy: a qualitative study. BMC pregnancy and childbirth, 13, 60. **https://doi.org/10.1186/1471-2393-13-60**

2. Society for Personality and Social Psychology. (2012, June 12). A father's love is one of the greatest influences on personality development. SCIENCEDAILY. Retrieved October 8, 2020 from **www.sciencedaily.com/releases/2012/06/120612101338.htm**

3. J. Rosenberg, W. Bradford Wilcox, Ph.D., (2006), U.S. Department of Health and Human Services Administration for Children and families, Child Abuse and Neglect User Manual Series: The Importance of Fathers in the Healthy Development of Children.

Layer Three – Delayed Growth

1. https://www.researchgate.net/publication/6695257_Father_absence_and_adolescent_development_A_review_of_the_literature.

2. East L, Jackson D, O'Brien L. Father absence and adolescent development: a review of the literature. Journal of Child Health Care. 2006;10(4):283-295. doi:10.1177/1367493506067869

   Trickett PK, Noll JG, Putnam FW. The impact of sexual abuse on female development: lessons from a multigenerational, longitudinal research study. Dev Psychopathol. 2011;23(2):453-476. doi:10.1017/S0954579411000174

Layer Six – Shame, Rejection, and Guilt

1. Rejection - Excerpted from God's Remedy for Rejection by Derek Prince, © 1993, 2019 by Derek Prince Ministries–International. Published by Whitaker House, New Kensington, PA. Used with permission. All rights reserved. **www.whitakerhouse.com**.

2. Rejection - John Eckhardt, Destroying the Spirit of Rejection (Lake Mary, FL: Charisma House, 2006), Used by Permission.

www.ingramcontent.com/pod-product-compliance
Lightning Source LLC
Chambersburg PA
CBHW070155100426
42743CB00013B/2913